Inside Worry Free

Business Security 8.0

with Exchange

Administrator's Guide

Dale Johnson

Johnson Consulting Inc.

Inside WFBS 8.0

ISBN: 978-1-300-64358-6

Johnson Consulting, Inc. 21 Parliament Lane, Woburn MA 08101
www.jconsult.com 877-228-8595

Dale Johnson

Table of Contents

Chapter 1: Requirements and Installation
As of Version 8.0

Changes from WFBS 7.0

Removed from program

- DHCP Login checks removed from Vulnerability scanner. But you can always keep your old version
- Agents no longer have the ability to scan network drives and shares.
- No longer supported OS: , Media Center 2005, XP SP2 (upgrade to SP3)
- TMTouch tool is removed.

Additions to program

- Windows 8 Support
- Windows Server 2012 Support
- Trusted Programs: You can now add programs to the trusted list and stop the WFBS Agent from looking at anything they do.
- Everything runs on IPv6 along with IPv4
- Exchange (Messaging Agent) now has DLP lite. OfficeScan has a bit more DLP, and DLP Heavy has all the DLP you can ever want.
- You can now make all your workstations and servers shutdown after their scheduled scan. I bet that could be dangerous!
- FakeAV like programs now have the option to "Run Advanced Cleanup" during scans. You should turn this on to stop the nasty Anti-virus killing programs. The option is in your scan settings. USE IT!
- Content Filtering on Exchange now allows you to place the files in a separate archive for each rule.
- 2 new tools allow you to regenerate the Agents GUID and uninstall the Agent.
- You can decide where exactly on your workstations and Servers to install the Agent.

Server Types: WFBS 8 Server now runs the following Windows Operating Systems (32 or 64 bit). It is recommended that if you have a Server you use that instead of a workstation style operating system. Also, do not combine WFBS with other server-like programs on a non-server OS, as WFBS does not respond favorably to this. Remember non-server OS's (OSi?) limit you to 10 connections at once. Note the Mac products need the Mac Plugin

- XP Professional/Home SP3 - (no IPv6) support
- Vista, all versions SP1/SP2
- Windows 7, all/no SPs
- Windows 8, RC 8400+
- Home Server, PP2/PP3 - (no IPv6) support
- Server 2003/R2, all versions SP1/SP2 - (no IPv6) support
- SBS 2003/R2 Server, SP1/SP2 - (no IPv6) support
- Storage Server 2003/R2 - (no IPv6) support
- Server 2008/R2, all versions SP1/SP2
- Server 2008 R2, all versions, no SP/SP1
- SBS 2008 Server, SP1/SP2
- Essential 2008, SP1/SP2
- Storage Server 2008
- SBS 2011 Standard no, SP/SP1
- SBS 2011 Essentials no, SP1
- Home Server 2011, SP1
- Server 2012, RC8400+
- Mac OS X Snow Leopard 10.6+ - (no IPv6) support
- Mac OS X Leopard 10.5.7+ - (no IPv6) support
- Mac OS X Tiger 10.4.11+ - (no IPv6) support

WFBS **WILL NOT** run on Server Cores.

Agent Installs: The WFBS Agent will work on all the Operating Systems noted above plus all versions of Windows 7 and Windows XP. Overall, WFBS will protect any operating systems since Windows XP and 2003 were released.   The Agent will need an extra 350MB of disk space on each workstation if using Smart Scanning and 800MB+ if using conventional scanning.   Memory needed to run the WFBS Agent depends on the OS type; this does not mean that you need this much extra memory, just that you need this much memory already installed on the workstation/server. Note the Mac products need the Mac Plugin.

- XP Professional/Home SP3 - (no IPv6) support

- Vista, all versions SP1/SP2
- Windows 7, all/no SPs
- Windows 8, RC 8400+
- Home Server, PP2/PP3 - (no IPv6) support
- Server 2003/R2, all versions SP1/SP2 - (no IPv6) support
- SBS 2003/R2 Server, SP1/SP2   - (no IPv6) support
- Storage Server 2003/R2   - (no IPv6) support
- Server 2008/R2, all versions SP1/SP2
- Server 2008 R2, all versions, no SP/SP1
- SBS 2008 Server, SP1/SP2
- Essential 2008, SP1/SP2
- Storage Server 2008
- SBS 2011 Standard no, SP/SP1
- SBS 2011 Essentials no, SP1
- Home Server 2011, SP1
- Server 2012, RC8400+
- Mac OS X Snow Leopard 10.6+ - (no IPv6) support
- Mac OS X Leopard 10.5.7+ - (no IPv6) support
- Mac OS X Tiger 10.4.11+ - (no IPv6) support
- Mac: OS X Mountain Lion 10.8+ - (no IPv6) support
- Mac OS X Lion 10.7+ - (no IPv6) support

Replacing other Antivirus: WFBS will make its best attempt to automatically uninstall the following antivirus programs for you. The biggest reason for failure of this feature is that the initial install of the antivirus program did not use default settings or was an upgrade from a previous version. If by chance you find that you have a large group of machines that will not uninstall, Trend Micro Support can usually create you an uninstallation template if you have the original installation package of the old product. The products it can automatically uninstall include:

- Trend Micro Internet security 2008+, OfficeScan 8+, Titanium 1.0+
- Norton CE 8.0+, Symantec 2008+
- McAfee VirusScan, ASaP, SpamKiller, Security Center: 7+
- LANDesk VirusProtect 5.0
- CA eTrust 6.0+, InocuLAN 5, iTechnology iGateway 4.0+
- PANDA 6.0+, NT, 2004+
- F-Secure 4.04+, Backweb, Client Security 7.1, 2008+, for Workstations 7.11
- Kaspersky 6.0+, 2009+
- Microsoft Onecare 2.0, Forefront 1.0+
- Sophos NT 5.0+, 9X+
- Others : Ahnlab, Authentium, Amrein, Grisoft, ViRobot, Tegem.....

IPv4 and IPv6: If you are going to use both IPv4 and IPv6 on the server you must use the Host name as the name of the server and not either of the IP addresses. This will allow both IP systems to look up the server in DNS, instead of trying to reach an IP address it might not have.

IPv6: You can only install on server with IPv6 on:

- 2008 Server.
- 2008 SBS.
- 2012 Server.
- 2011 SBS.
- Windows 7
- Windows 8
- Widows Vista

Memory: You should consider 1GB for your server and 1GB for WFBS (so 2GB Total). If you use Windows 2008 servers, you may want to consider 4GB, as the operating system itself uses much more memory than older operating systems. Windows 2011 servers? Double it again. We want a good 8GB now. Saying that, I have never seen it take that much memory. But Trend Micro claims it has happened with Smart Scan turned on. So make your choice.

Inside of RAM

To determine how much RAM you have installed and are using (or not using) on your server you can simply check your Task Manager. You can easily pull up your Task Manager by clicking on CRTL+SHIFT+ESC at the same time. Click on the Performance tab. Under physical Memory you will find Total memory and Available Memory. In my example I have 3.14GB (3GB) and 1.3GB of free memory. When we say you need 1GB of RAM, this means at its peak, the program will utilize 1GB of RAM. This is not something that will happen all the time. So if you're close or a bit over, odds are this won't be a terrible thing. If you only have 500MB of free RAM then maybe you need to consider that to be a problem.

Totals		Physical Memory (K)	
Handles	31113	Total	3143760
Threads	918	Available	1327696
Processes	77	System Cache	1112200

Commit Charge (K)		Kernel Memory (K)	
Total	1561936	Total	224712
Limit	5074016	Paged	176328
Peak	2217000	Nonpaged	48384

Disk Space: Trend Micro recommends 6GB, which is a little low; the installation itself takes 2.5GB. The pattern files are the killer; they can take up a good 6MB if you are using Smart Scanning. Depending on the amount of users you have, you will need between 500MB and 3GB of disk space. A quick method for estimating what you need is to start at 2.5GB and add 100MB for each user you are connecting to your system. If you already have the 9GB free then use it, and don't worry about it. If you have less, you should consider what drive you install WFBS on.

Service Packs and Security Updates: If you are running a Windows server, YOU MUST keep your server up to date on Service Packs and security updates. If you're up to date, you have nothing to worry about when installing new software. If you're not, Trend Micro does list Service Pack requirements in the ReadMe file with WFBS.

V-ware: You can use WFBS on systems running VMware ESX 3.0/3.5+, VMware Server 1.0.3/2.0.1+ , VMware Workstation 6/0/6.5+ or Microsoft Hyper-V Server 2008.

Web Server: All Windows servers utilize IIS. WFBS will work with IIS6+ (again, it must be patched and service packed). If you use XP, you can setup IIS on the XP machine. With Vista you will have to take the Apache option. You can use Apache (included with the install) on any server you wish, although I have seen problems using the WFBS install of Apache when you already run IIS on a server. I would recommend a separate install of Apache before installing WFBS on Apache.

Your Exchange Server Needs

If you're running Exchange server 2003 SP2, 2007 SP1, or 2010 SP1/2 and purchased the option to protect it, you will need to consider a few things. Exchange can be installed on either the same server as WFBS or a different server. Lots of small companies run multiple products on the same server and combining WFBS with Exchange and other products is just fine. WFBS really does not use a lot of the server utilization and bandwidth. About the only time you will utilize a good deal of utilization is during a virus outbreak where you have to update and communicate to your workstations to help resolve the problem you are having. In this case you will utilize as much of the server as you need to, and you will not be worrying that the other items on the server having slowed down.

The Exchange option will install separate software on your exchange server and will need to utilize 1GB of Ram.

For disk space, expect to use 2GB of disk space ON the exchange server itself. The addition of disk space to the WFBS server is minimal and doesn't need to be considered. Running out of disk space on an Exchange server is a VERY BAD thing. Always make sure your exchange server and the drive the exchange server lives on have plenty of disk space.

Dale Johnson

Thoughts on doing Installs, Upgrading or Uninstalling WFBS

Going from an Evaluation to Full version

1. Go to Preferences –> Product License -> View License Upgrade Instructions.
2. Click online registration and type in your registration key and select activate.

Upgrade

- You will need to reboot? Agents -almost always. Servers- 50/50.
- You can only upgrade directly from WFBS 5.0, 5.1, 6.0, or 7.0. If you have a lower version of CSM you should probably consider uninstalling your old program and installing the new program fresh. If you're on WFBS 5 or 6, is your server too old to upgrade and use anymore? This is a chance to think about it.
- Do you have virtualized servers?   This might be a chance to remove a physical server and go Virtual.
- In your WFBS was on Server 2000, nope it isn't going to work anymore.
- You can't upgrade a previous install of OfficeScan or Scan Mail for Exchange to WFBS. If you have these programs you should contact support about possible options.
    - Downgrade from OfficeScan
        - Uninstall OfficeScan completely
        - Run the new WFBS install
        - Uninstall each Agent, and reinstall with new WFBS Agent
    - Downgrade from ScanMail
        - Uninstall ScanMail completely
        - Run the new WFBS install
- Upgrade from CSM 3.0/3.5/3.6
    - Uninstall CSM completely
    - Run the new WFBS install
    - Uninstall each Agent, and reinstall with new WFBS Agent
- Upgrade from Messaging 3.0/3.5/3.6
    - Uninstall CSM MGA completely (possibly using the manual uninstall for ScanMail)
    - Run the new WFBS install
- Upgrade from WFBS 5.0/5.1 - **We recommend a complete uninstall and reinstall.**
    - Can your server handle more memory and utilization?
    - Will upgrade both server and exchange (MSA) server.
    - Backup your data (don't trust the upgrade to do it) - http://esupport.trendmicro.com/Pages/Important-files-to-back-up-before-upgrading-to-Worry-Free-Business-Sec.aspx
    - Remove Exchange log files older than 0 days, old log files will not be migrated into the program anyway.
    - Run the install and pick upgrade.

- Upgrade from WFBS 6.0
    - Can your server handle more memory and utilization?
    - Will upgrade both server and Exchange (MSA) server.
    - Backup your data (don't trust the upgrade to do it) - http://esupport.trendmicro.com/Pages/Important-files-to-back-up-before-upgrading-to-Worry-Free-Business-Sec.aspx
    - Remove Exchange log files older than 0 days, old log files will not be migrated into the program anyway.
    - Run the install and pick upgrade.
- Upgrade from WFBS 7.0
    - Will upgrade both server and Exchange (MSA) server.
    - Backup your data (don't trust the upgrade to do it) - http://esupport.trendmicro.com/Pages/Important-files-to-back-up-before-upgrading-to-Worry-Free-Business-Sec.aspx
    - Remove Exchange log files older than 0 days, old log files will not be migrated into the program anyway.
    - Run the install and pick upgrade.

Reinstall

- You will need to reboot.
- If you need to do a manual uninstall there are technotes on Trend Micro's technote website.

Uninstall

- If you installed WFBS with the default setup you should be able to use *Add or Remove Programs* to uninstall the program.
- You WILL need to know the WFBS administrator password to uninstall the server automatically. If you do not know it you will need to do a manual uninstall.
- If you used Apache you will have leftover data in the Apache server, and the Apache server will not be uninstalled.
- Clients WILL NOT be uninstalled during an uninstall of WFBS. You have a few options to uninstall the actual clients. REMOVING CLIENTS is dangerous if you do not have a replacement program.
    - If the server is still running you can select Uninstall the Selected Agents from the Security Settings, Remove option in the web console.
    - If the server has been uninstalled - You need either to use your replacement programs to uninstall or uninstall the program via the workstation's *Add or Remove Programs*.
    - If you do the uninstall on the workstations you will need to know the uninstall password.
    - WFBS has an Uninstall tool you can use to uninstall the Clients. You just better find it before you uninstall WFBS and it gets deleted. See the Tools Chapter.
- The Exchange part (MSA) will not be uninstalled. You must follow the ScanMail (MSA) uninstall technotes to remove it.

- The manual uninstall (if you need to run it) will need you to use Regedit, if you do not feel comfortable using this program, please find a consultant who is.

Remote Install (installing from someplace other than the server)

- Remote install won't work on XP Home
- On XP machines, simple File Sharing must be turned off
- On Vista or Windows 7, make sure the remote registry service is turned on, and File and Print Sharing must be turned on via the Windows Firewall
- We recommend installing WFBS from the server itself. This way you can see (feel) problems before they get out of control. You should only do remote installs if you feel very safe about the server you are installing on and have the knowledge to deal with problems via some kind of remote control.

Things to think about and data needed ahead of time for install

- Download the software from http://www.trendmicro.com/download
- Do you already have another anti-virus installed on the server? It needs to be uninstalled before you start installing WFBS. Anti-virus programs do not get along with each other.
- Server Install Location (See the requirements we already talked about)
    - IP address *(?.?.?.?)* Does the server have more than one IP address?
    - IPv6 and IPv4. You can utilize WFBS before you implement IPv6, but please use the Host Name and not the IPv4 IP address for the Agents to phone home.
    - Server name *(host and domain name)*
    - Disk drive you want to install the program on *(?:)*
        - Server Operating System
        - Service Packs up to date
        - Critical updates complete
    - Username and password of an account that has administrative rights on your server, or simply your domain admin username and password
    - SMTP location. If you have an exchange server, then you would use the IP address of that server. If you outsource your mail server, then use the IP address of that server. If you use Hotmail or Gmail or such, then you won't be using this option.
    - Do you have IIS installed and running? If you don't know if IIS is installed, then you can check by going to (on the server) Add/Remove Programs for the Control Panel. Click on Add/Remove Windows Components on the left side. Look for IIS in the list of components that appears and see if it's selected. If not selected then you will need to follow the Microsoft technotes for your Server Type to install IIS, or you can use the Apache option that comes with WFBS, and install it either before hand with separate Apache install code (best bet), or use the Apache install in the WFBS install itself.
- Number of Clients to install WFBS on.
    - Operating Systems Clients/Servers you will install the Client on.
    - Do you have groups of clients (Accounting, HR, Manufacturing...?) List those groups.
- Network setup.

- o Do you have Mobile (always) users? This means the user's machine NEVER connects to your network. Examples are home machines, off-site offices. How many?
- o Do you have Traveling users, who spend at least occasional time out of the office with their computer? How many and how often do they connect?
- o Do you have users who live on the other side of the Internet or use the Internet over a very slow connection? How many and how do they connect to your office?
- Exchange Server? (See the requirements already talked about)
  - o IP address *(?.?.?.?)*
  - o Server name
  - o Disk drive you want to install the program on *(?:)*
  - o Server Operating System
    - ▪ Service Packs up to date
    - ▪ Critical updates complete
- Don't run an install in a terminal session. It will cause the install to be.. well terminal.
- Do you already use Trend Micro Web Protection Add-On? Remove it first.
- These ports must be open to use on the server. HTTP: 8059, SSL: 4343 and 4345

Upgrading from Client Server Messaging (CSM)

If you cannot directly upgrade because you have an older version of WFBS (called Client Server Messaging) you will need to uninstall the whole program from the server and install WFBS 8 fresh. Since you have this option you should consider a few things:

- Is the server stable and will it last another few years?
- Does the server have enough drive space and memory?
- Have I bought another server recently that this might work better on?
- Should I consider using a virtual server?

Agents: When uninstalling you will NOT be uninstalling the Agents themselves, just the server. This means you will have to uninstall each Agent and upgrade it to WFBS 8. If you are going to do this, you must consider that if you had upgraded WFBS every 1-2 years as upgrades become available, you would not have to make such drastic changes; they would be automated.

Exchange: If you have the Exchange Agent installed (MSA) you will be asked for the administrative username and password to uninstall the Exchange agent. You cannot install the new MSA unless the old one is uninstalled, so this must be done.

Settings: No settings will be kept from CSM and that probably is not a bad thing. You will have to setup the program from scratch, and use the default settings until you find any changes you might need. If you know your install was special and not close to default, a bunch of screen shots of the console before uninstalling might be a smart thing to do.

Dale Johnson

Downloading

Download the latest install package from *www.trendmicro.com/download*. Make sure to pick the correct version of WFBS as Standard and Advanced have different install programs.

Run *WFBS80_EN_GM_B???.exe* which is not the install program itself, but the Trend Micro downloader.

Clicking start will download the correct install files.

- If you select begin installation, after download completes, it will start the installation.
- If you want the download to be placed in the same directory as the downloader program you will need to do nothing.
- If you want the install to be placed in a different directory, click the Set Path button and select the directory
- Once downloaded, the install program can be moved around and used on its own. Therefore you do not need to run the downloader on the server itself, but we recommend it.

Upgrading in Place.

Backup your old WFBS files.

We highly recommend backing up your old WFBS data with the following steps.

- Stop the Trend Micro Security Master Service

Trend Micro Security Server Master Service   Provides th...   Started   Automatic

- Make a copy of your HTTDB directory, usually located in your Program Files\Trend Micro\Security Server\PCCSRV directory.

   C:\Program Files\Trend Micro\Security Server\PCCSRV\HTTPDB

- Start the Trend Micro Security Master Service

Trend Micro Security Server Master Service   Provides th...   Started   Automatic

- If you have Hard Drive space issues you should also delete your old log files via your current console under Reports -> Maintenance ->Manual Log Deletion

Start the Upgrade

Either the program will have started the install for you or you should run the installer.

The program will now expand the data files onto your hard drive in the same location as the installer program. If you need disk space or to change the location, click on the browse button to make the change. The expansion of the files will take at least 1.2GB of disk space.

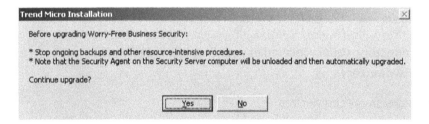

- This is a warning that this upgrade will use a decent amount of system resources and you should consider making sure the computer is ready for it.
- Also, the Current Agent on the server will be uninstalled and reinstalled during the upgrade.

The upgrade will now start with the expansion of the data and you can watch the screen and the bar until it finishes.

(When to update)

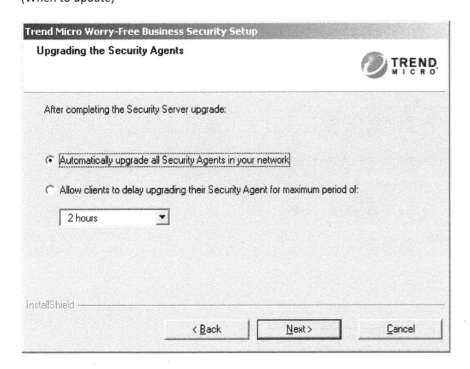

When the install is complete all of the Agents will need to be upgraded. This upgrade will consist of an uninstall of the old Agent and a reinstall of the new agent. This will slow down the workstations they are on. This might also cause the user to reboot the machine. We are now asked if we want to do this upgrade right away or delay it up to 24 hours.

- If a machine is offline at the time of the upgrade and is not turned on until after the delay period has completed, they will then get the upgrade when the workstation completely turns on and is communicating to the server.
- If you want to turn off upgrades and handle them by hand in the console , you can go into Security Settings -> Workstations -> Agent Configuration -> Client Privileges -> Update Settings

- **Disable program upgrade and hot fix deployment**: This will stop all upgrade from going from the server down to the client. Turning this back on will then send the updates to all the computers in the system.

Exchange

(If you have WFBS Advanced and Exchange)

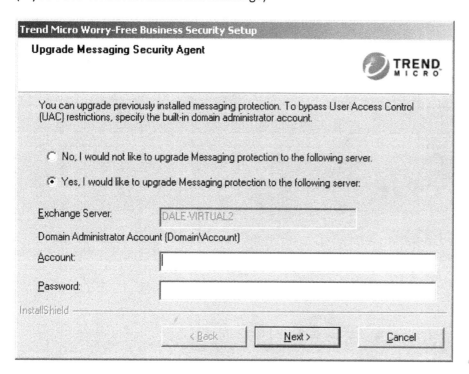

You will need to input your Exchange Administrative username (with domain like - insidewfbs80\administrator) and password to upgrade your Exchange server. You have the ability to skip the Exchange upgrade during the main upgrade process.   So, it's best to get it done right here.

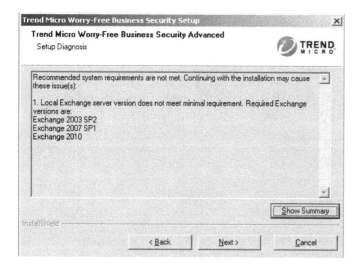

If your exchange environment is not up to date, you will receive this error screen. Note that WFBS does not work with Exchange 2000 at all.   Upgrade your Exchange to the desired level before WFBS can continue. This is probably a good thing to do no matter if you are installing WFBS or not.

Inside Exchange Versions: How do you find your exchange version? Best bet is to go to the Exchange System Manager (Start -> Programs -> Microsoft Exchange ->System Manager) -> Help -> About Exchange System.

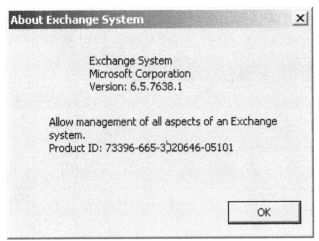

But how do you turn that into what service pack you are using?   On the Internet search for "Microsoft 158530" The search should bring up a link to a technote called "Build numbers and release dates for Exchange Server - Microsoft " You can then take your build number (in 6.5.7226 the build number is 7226) and cross reference it to find out what SP of Exchange you have running. If this scares you, then please contact your IT consultant about the upgrade.

The Update

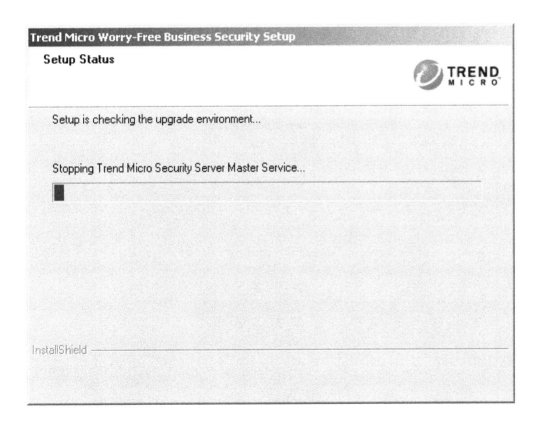

The upgrade begins. This is a good chance to go get some coffee and a snack, because the upgrade will take some time. If you're doing an Exchange upgrade also, you might consider lunch or dinner.

The setup has completed and now you have the options to:

- **Launch the console**
- **Install the Remote Manager Agent.** You will have been given the information needed to run this install from your reseller if you are going to use this option.
- **Read the ReadMe.** If you're the readme type.

Let's start by running the install of WFBS you downloaded from Trend Micro. We will go step by step with screen shots to explain the questions that are being asked.

1. **License agreement.** Read it or not, you will still need to say accept to continue.

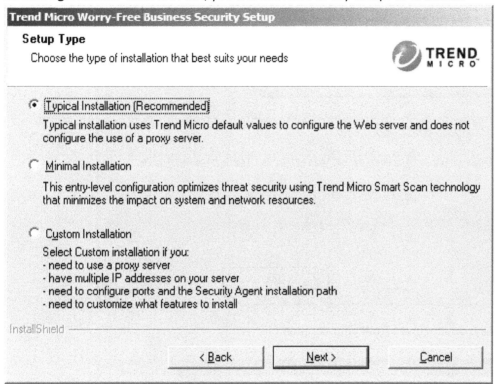

2. Are we going to do a typical installation, Minimal or a custom installation?   Unless you know you have something special you need to setup (disk drive, web server…) we recommend the typical install.
    1. Reasons to choose a Minimal install:
        i. You are only going to use Anti-virus and Anti-spyware.
    2. Reasons to choose a Custom install:
        i. Using Apache instead of IIS.
        ii. Using an IIS website other than the default website.
        iii. To stop the pre-scan of the server.
        iv. Choosing non-typical ports for the server to use.
        v. Not using a domain.
        vi. Using a Proxy Server for the communication of the server.
        vii. You will be using An IP address instead of a HOST name to communicate between the Agents and the Server.
        viii. You use IPv6 along with IPv4.

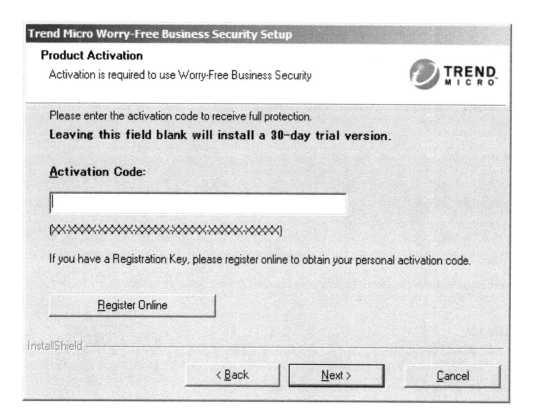

3. Type in the keys you received from your reseller

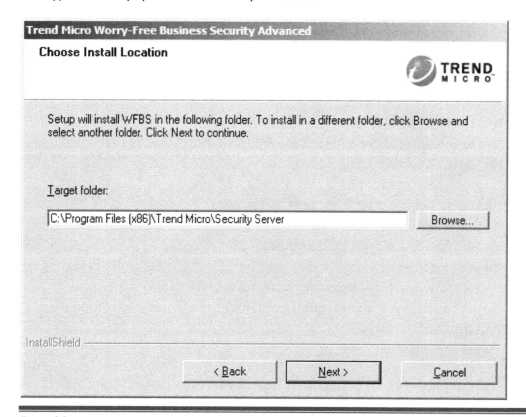

4. **Target Directory.** Where on the server do you want the program installed to? Some servers are built so that only the operating system goes on the C drive. Others have no special setup and all you care about is the amount of disk space you have available. Just don't pick a drive that's going empty.

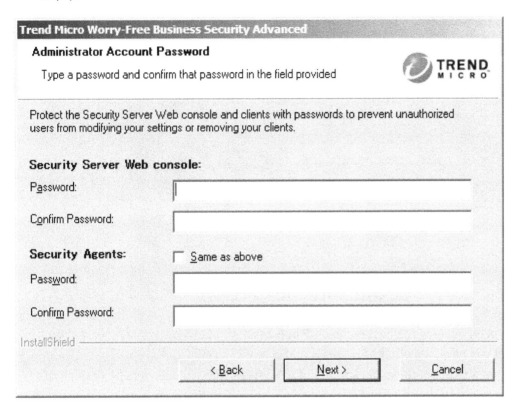

5. **Passwords.** Passwords are important and MUST be written down. There are 2 passwords, the first is the password used to login to the server web console and uninstall the product. The second is the Agent password used to uninstall or stop the agent process on your workstations or servers. DO NOT use the same passwords for security sake and DO NOT lose these passwords, or uninstalling the software will be a burden. DO NOT CLICK the same as above button for any reason!

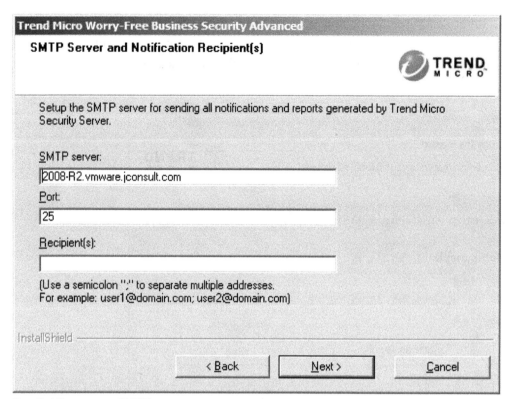

6. **Setting up an SMTP server**.
   1. Here we need to know the host name or IP address of the SMTP server we talked about earlier. If you have none that's fine.
   2. We also need to put in the email address of the person who would like to be notified of problems found by the system. If the Exchange server is on the same machine, you can just keep the auto fill information on the screen.

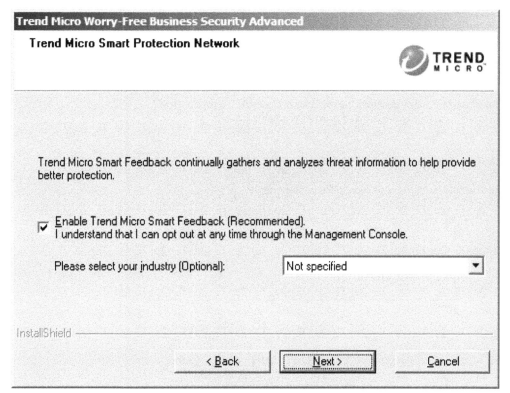

7. Do you want to join the Trend Micro Smart Network? Trend Micro uses this system to help determine what viruses are in the world, where they are located around the globe and prepare emergency responses to attacks. You can also see this information at http://us.trendmicro.com/us/trendwatch. There is no real loss by saying yes; you will not be giving any data that will hurt your organization with this being enabled.

If you are not installing the Exchange MSA jump to the 'Finish the Install' to continue with the install.

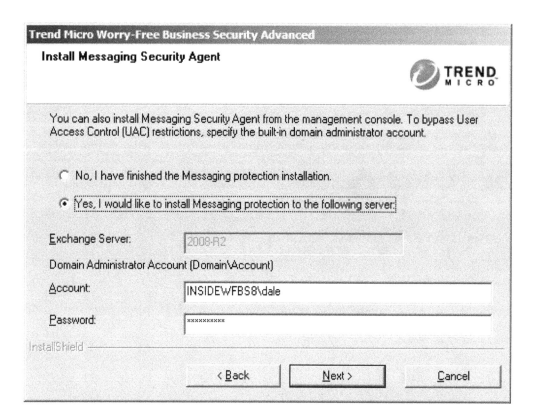

8. You will need to input credentials for an account that has Domain and Exchange Administrative rights.

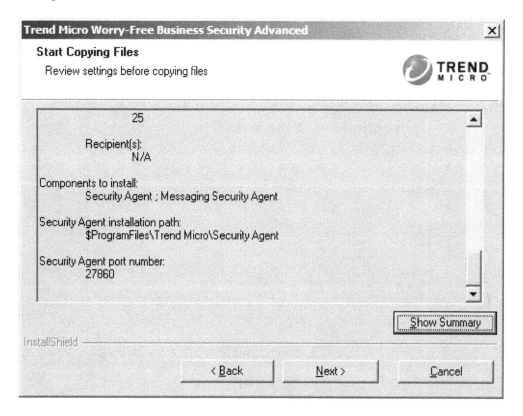

9. WFBS will now show you a list of what it has found about your Exchange server and what it is going to do to install the MSA. There is a 'Show Summary' Button 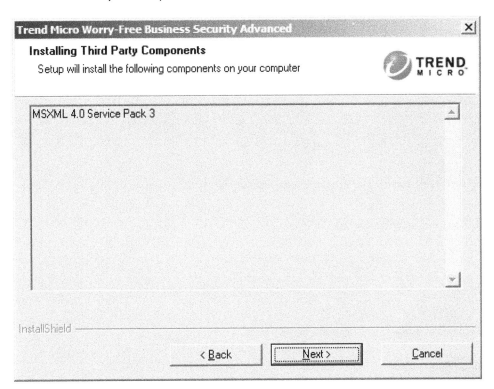 if you would like to open this summary in Notepad and save it.

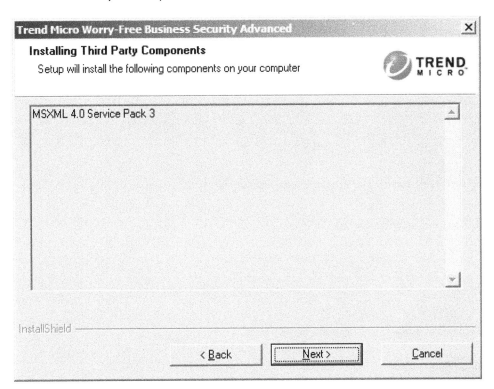

10. If there are other programs which WFBS must install to complete the installation they will be listed.

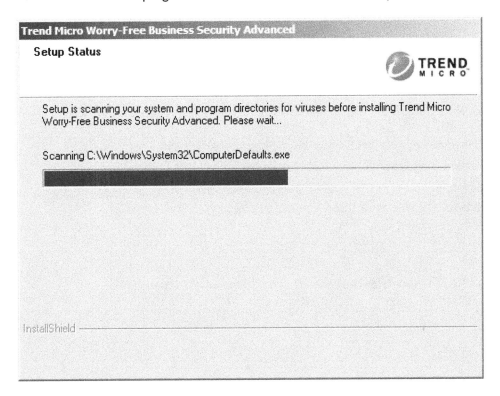

11. Installation of the WFBS begins with both the Exchange and full server installs, have a cup of coffee and come on back in 5-15 minutes or so.

Coffee break time.....

You are done. The WFBS server should have installed along with the web console. If you requested the MSA installation, that should be done too. You have a few choices here to get you started.

a. **Launch the Console:** Let's start this baby up and start cooking.
b. **Install the Remote Manager Agent**. You will have been given the information needed to run this install from your reseller if you are going to use this option.
c. **View the Readme:** If your one of those types of people.

Jump to the 'Finish the Install' to continue with the install.

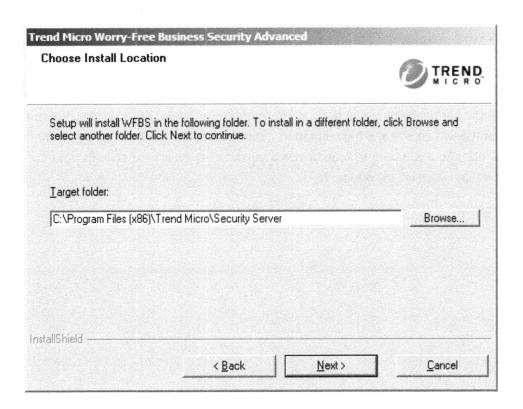

Trend Micro Worry-Free Business Security Setup

Product Activation
Activation is required to use Worry-Free Business Security

TREND MICRO

Please enter the activation code to receive full protection.
Leaving this field blank will install a 30-day trial version.

Activation Code:

(XX-XXXX-XXXXX-XXXXX-XXXXX-XXXXX-XXXXX)

If you have a Registration Key, please register online to obtain your personal activation code.

Register Online

InstallShield

< Back   Next >   Cancel

1. Type in the keys you received from your reseller.

Trend Micro Worry-Free Business Security Advanced

Choose Install Location

TREND MICRO

Setup will install WFBS in the following folder. To install in a different folder, click Browse and select another folder. Click Next to continue.

Target folder:

C:\Program Files (x86)\Trend Micro\Security Server   Browse...

InstallShield

< Back   Next >   Cancel

2. **Target Directory.** Where on the server do you want the program installed to? Some servers are built so that only the operating system goes on the C drive. Others have no special setup and all you care about is the amount of disk space you have available. Just don't pick a drive that's not going to have enough space. A quick note about Apache. If you are installing Apache, it will install in the same drive as you select here, so make sure you have space for both Apache and WFBS in this instance.

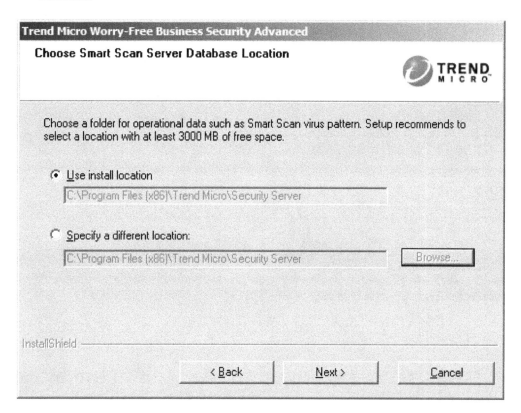

3. **Smart Scan Server Database Location.** Here we can choose either to install the Smart Scan Server Database along with the normal WFBS server or on a different drive or server. Why would you want to pick a different location? Disk size and fragmentation. This location will be used more than the normal WFBs server files. So if you want to keep this on a separate psychical hard drive for speed and fragmentation reasons you should consider it.

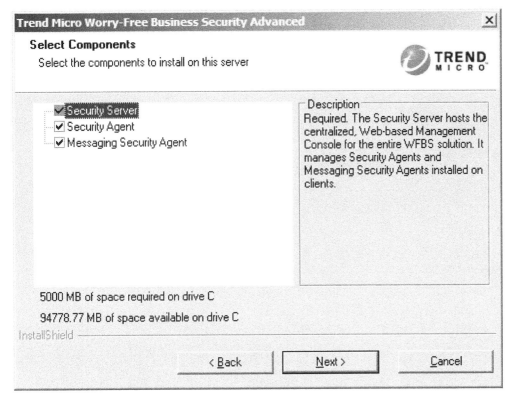

4. What components do you want to install?

- **Security Server:** Will install the WFBS Server on the server. This option should always be selected.
- **Server Agent:** Will install the Agent onto the server itself. This is very important and will make sure that WFBS can't be taken over by attacks. You should always choose this option.
- **Messaging Security Agent (MSA):** If you have Exchange installed on the same server as you are installing WFBS you will automatically have this option selected. WFBS install will then install the MSA after installing the server side of WFBS. There is little reason not to select this option here and save yourself some time later on. If you DO NOT want to install the MS agent on the C: drive of the Exchange Server DO NOT run this option now, as it is hard coded into this part of the installation.

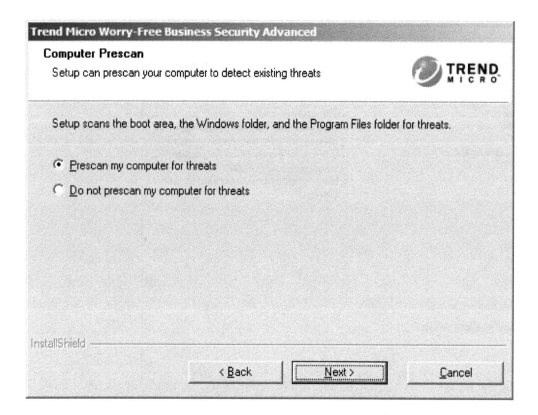

5. WFBS will now scan your server to make sure there isn't a prevailing problem with it. Installing anti-virus software on a server that is already infected will probably cause the install to fail or not do its job. PLEASE PRESCAN!

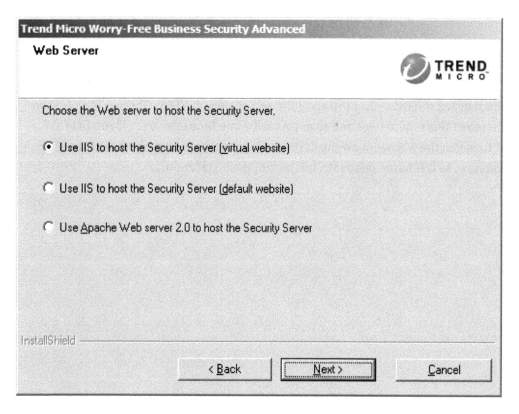

Dale Johnson

6. Would you like to install the web console on IIS or Apache?
   a. If you do not have IIS already installed you will not have the option to use it. In this case if you want to use IIS, you must stop the install, and install IIS on the server.
   b. As mentioned before the Apache option will install Apache on your server. In the past we have seen a few problems doing this on an older (used) server and recommend installing the server first on your own instead of using the Trend Micro option for a full install. If the server is new then there shouldn't be a problem with the Apache install.

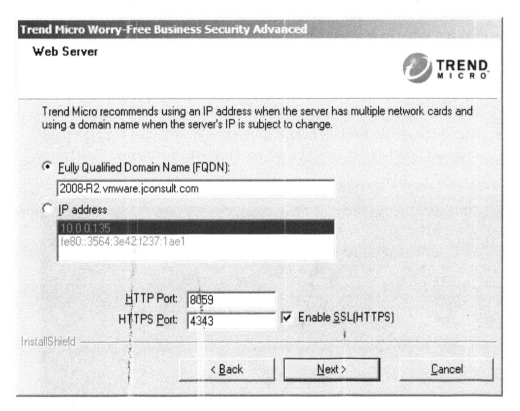

6. **What Server?** The next question determines what server information you have for the server you will be installing on. Since you are running this install on the server itself, the information would already be filled in. Now we must make a major decision! Will we allow the clients to communicate to the server via Domain (Host name) or IP address? The answer to this question has a few areas of thought you must consider.
   - **IPv4 and IPv6**: If you are going to use both IPv4 and IPv6 on the server you must use the Host name as the name of the server and not either of the IP address. This will allow both IP systems to look up the server in DNS
   - **Domain (Host) name.** If you use the Domain and Host name then your DNS MUST be setup, and be seen by all your clients. How do you know if this is true? See the information in the field next to Domain name? Write that down; go to another machine (or three) on your network. Go to **START -> RUN.** Type in **CMD** into the box that appears and enter.

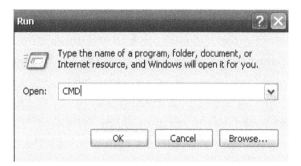

A nice black box will appear where you should then type.
PING FIELD.INFO.YOU.WROTE.DOWN

- If your machine shows a REPLY from the device (as in the first example below), then your clients can connect to the server using the Domain (Host) name.
- If (as in the second example below) you receive an error that the pin request could not find the Host, then you will not be able to use Domain (Host) name

```
C:\WINDOWS\system32\cmd.exe

Microsoft Windows XP [Version 5.1.2600]
(C) Copyright 1985-2001 Microsoft Corp.

C:\Documents and Settings\dale.JC2009>ping jc2k32009.jc2009.local

Pinging jc2k32009.jc2009.local [10.0.0.51] with 32 bytes of data:

Reply from 10.0.0.51: bytes=32 time<1ms TTL=128
Reply from 10.0.0.51: bytes=32 time<1ms TTL=128
Reply from 10.0.0.51: bytes=32 time<1ms TTL=128
Reply from 10.0.0.51: bytes=32 time<1ms TTL=128

Ping statistics for 10.0.0.51:
    Packets: Sent = 4, Received = 4, Lost = 0 (0% loss),
Approximate round trip times in milli-seconds:
    Minimum = 0ms, Maximum = 0ms, Average = 0ms

C:\Documents and Settings\dale.JC2009>ping jc2k32011.jc2009.local
Ping request could not find host jc2k32011.jc2009.local. Please check the name a
nd try again.
```

- If you use the IP address option, this will enable your machines to connect to the server via the IP address, which in 99% of the networks out there should happen by default. The only problem with this option is if in the future you change the IP address of the server, the clients will not be automatically updated with the new info. You will have to go to each machine to make an update.

Enabling SSL: Do you want to use HTTPS when you connect to your WFBS Console? We recommend you do this, as it adds a layer of safety. This will mean that instead of using :8060 in your console web address you will use :4344.

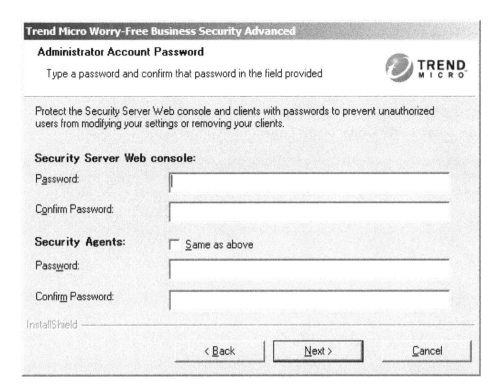

7. **Passwords.** Passwords are important and MUST be written down. There are two passwords; the first is the password used to login to the server web console and uninstall the server. The second is the Agent password used to uninstall or stop the agent process on your workstations or servers. DO NOT use the same passwords for security's sake and DO NOT lose these passwords, or uninstalling the software will be a burden. Do not click 'Same as Above'.

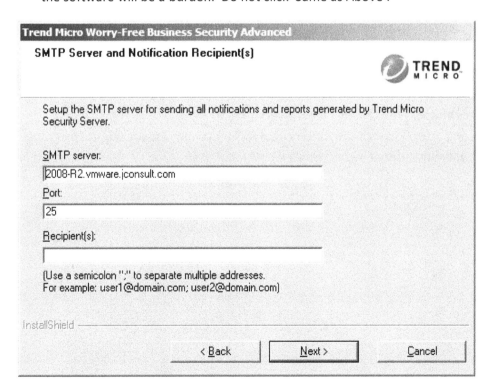

8. **Setting up an SMTP server.**
    a. Here we need to know the host name or IP address of the SMTP server we talked about earlier. If you have none that's fine.
    b. We also need to put in the email address of the person who would like to be notified of problems found by the system. If the exchange server is on the same machine you can just keep the auto fill information on the screen.

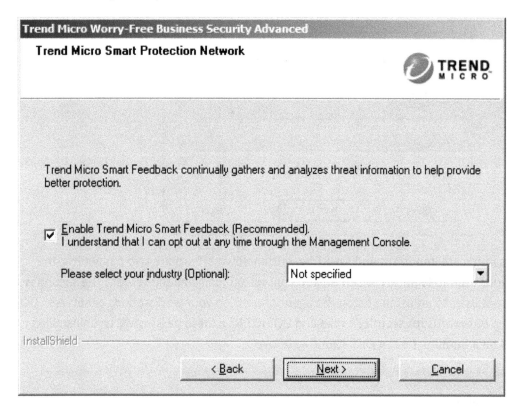

9. Do you want to join the Trend Micro Smart Network? Trend Micro uses this system to help determine what viruses are in the world, where they are located around the globe and prepare emergency responses to attacks. You can also see this information at http://us.trendmicro.com/us/trendwatch. There is no real loss by saying yes; you will not be giving any data that will hurt your organization with this being enabled.

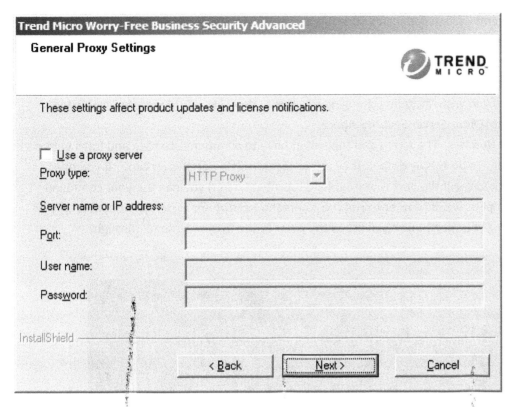

10. If you use a proxy server between your server and the Internet, please include that information here.

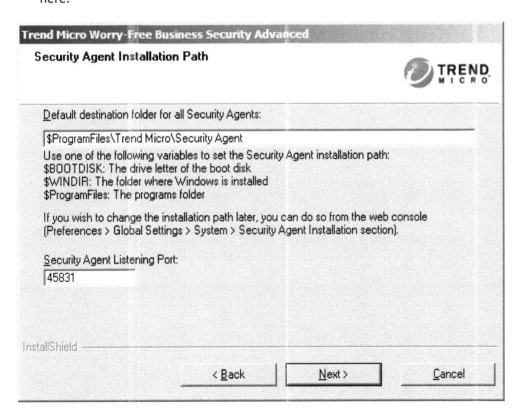

11. **Installing the Agent:** When you install your Agents we need to make two decisions.

   a. Where on your workstations would you like the Agents installed? By default we would use *$ProgramFiles\Trend Micro\Client Server Security Agent* which translate most the time to **C:\Program Files\Trend Micro\Client Server Security Agent.** You can change this if you wish, including changing to another drive like: *D:\Program Files\Trend Micro\Client Server Security Agent.*

   b. **Port Number**. The Agent and the Server have to communicate back and forth with each other. To do this by default they utilize the port listed on this screen. If you need to check to see if the port is utilized (and it probably isn't) you can use your command prompt as we did earlier to run the command *netstat –a.* It isn't the cleanest way of seeing your ports but it will list all the ports in use for you to scroll through.

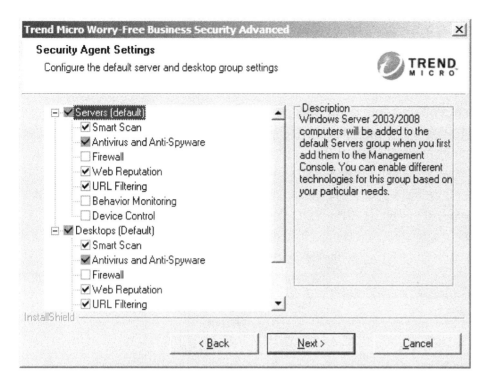

12. Now you can choose what parts of the program you would like install on each client during the first install process. This can all be changed afterward in the WFBS Console. We will talk about all these choices and why you might install or not install them in the Configuration chapter.

    c. Quick Installs. If you're interested in getting a quick install on your clients, and later getting them to update fully, you can select just *"Antivirus and Anti-Spyware"* now.

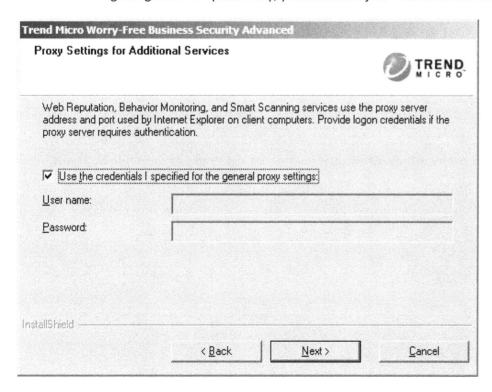

13. If you use a proxy server you are then asked for a General Proxy login. Parts of the WFBS agent need to utilize authentication to the proxy to verify the data they are getting. You can use the same credentials you already placed in for the server (even if there were no settings) if you select that option.

14. **Messaging Security Agent (MSA):** If you have Exchange installed on the same server as you are installing, WFBS you will automatically give you the MSA install questions next. WFBS install will then install the MSA after installing the server side of WFBS. You can follow along with that install as you read further. You will also need the administrator and password of the exchange administrator. The program will check to make sure it can log into with the information given, but WILL not check to make sure the login has the correct rights, so please check that yourself.

    • **Remote MSA:** If your exchange server is on a different server you will be able to install the exchange server after the install from your WFBS Console.

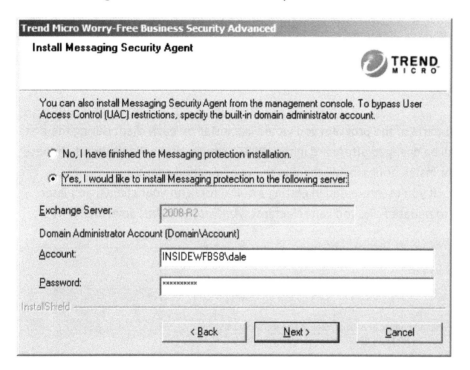

15. You will need to input credentials for an account that has Domain and Exchange Administrative rights.

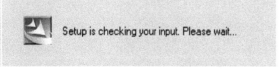

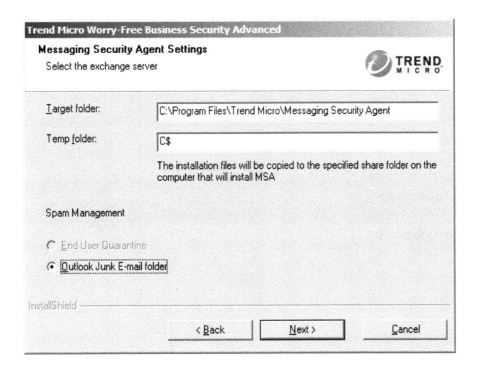

16. **Location to install the MSA**: If Exchange is on the same server as WFBS, where are we going to install the MSA program. By Default we will install it in the same location as the WFBS install, but you can change this to your liking.

17. **Spam Management:** This is only an option on Exchange 2003 servers. What folder do you want Junk mail to go into for Outlook.

      a. **End User Quarantine:** A special folder will be created in the users Outlook to hold the MSA's spam mail on Exchange 2003 servers..

      b. **Outlook Junk E-mail Folder:** Place all spam in the normal Outlook Junk mail folder. This is where all non-Exchange 2003 servers will put their spam mail.

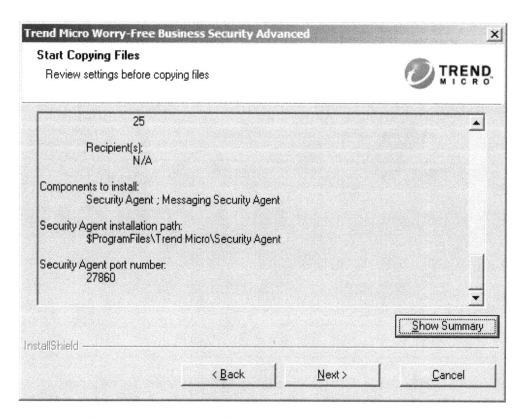

18. WFBS will now show you a list of what it has found about your Exchange server and what it is going to do to install the MSA. There is a 'Show Summary' Button Show Summary if you would like to open this summary in Notepad and save it.

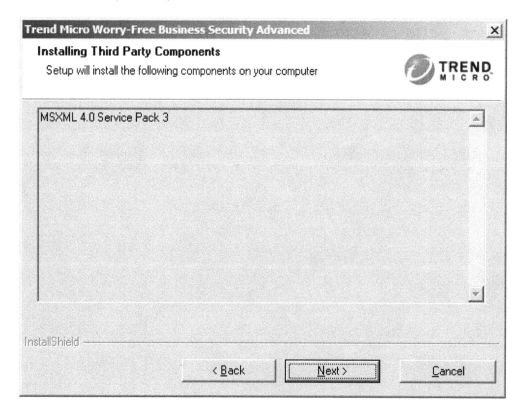

Dale Johnson

19. If there are other programs which WFBs must install to complete the installation they will be listed.

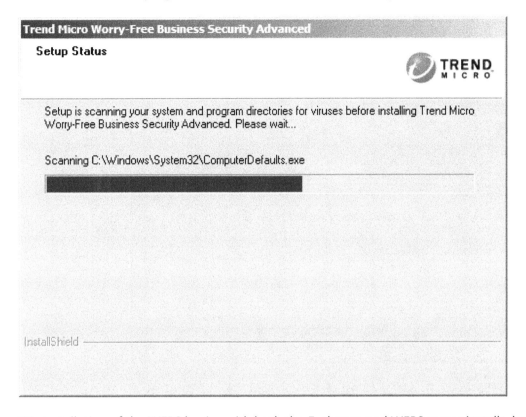

20. Installation of the WFBS begins with both the Exchange and WFBS server installs, have a cup of coffee and come on back in 5-15 minutes or so.

Coffee break time…..

Finish the Install

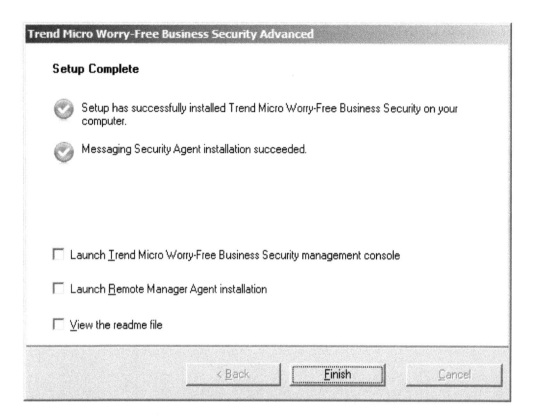

You are done. The WFBS server should have installed along with the web console. If you requested the MSA installation, that should be done too. You have a few choices here to get you started.

a. **Launch the Console:** Let's start this baby up and start cooking.
b. **Install the Remote Manager Agent**. You will have been given the information needed to run this install from your reseller if you are going to use this option.
c. **View the Readme**: If your one of those types of people.

Services: Once the install or upgrade is complete you will be able to continue your work. But it is best to check and make sure your services are running. Those services are:

○ For WFBS itself these services. Note you might not have all of them installed, depending on your setup.

Trend Micro Plug-in Manager	Installs an...	Started	Automatic	Local System
Trend Micro Security (for Mac)	Manages t...	Started	Automatic	Local System
Trend Micro Security Agent Listener	Facilitates ...		Automatic	Local System
Trend Micro Security Agent NT Proxy Service	Scans net...		Manual	Local System
Trend Micro Security Agent RealTime Scan	Security A...	Started	Automatic	Local System
Trend Micro Security Server Master Service	Provides th...	Started	Automatic	Local System
Trend Micro Smart Scan Service	Provides s...	Started	Manual	Local System
Trend Micro Unauthorized Change Preventi...	Manages t...		Manual	Local System

- For your WFBS MSA (Exchange). You should see all of these.

Trend Micro Messaging Security Agent EUQ ...	Messaging ...		Disabled	Local System
Trend Micro Messaging Security Agent Mast...	Messaging ...	Started	Automatic	Local System
Trend Micro Messaging Security Agent Rem...	Messaging ...		Disabled	Local System
Trend Micro Messaging Security Agent Syst...	Messaging ...	Started	Automatic	Local System

- And finally make sure your Exchange Services are started. Depending on what Exchange you are using and your setup... you could have any combination of services. Make sure the ones listed as Automatic on your system are started.

Opening the Console

By default these are the ports and address you selected in the install.

https://servername or ip:4343/SMB
http:// servername or ip:8059/SMB

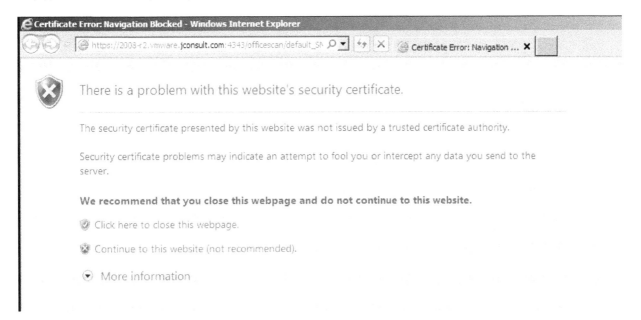

If you receive the following error it is because (like most of the small business world) you don; have certificates setup on your server. This is fine. You have 2 options to continue:

a. Click on "Continue to the website" and ignore the annoying Microsoft error. This shouldn't be a problem if your server is in your office and you know everything is secure. You will see this error every time you go to the console until you fix it. That's fine. If it doesn't bother you, it won't bother us any.

b. Fix the certificate problem. We used to describe how to here, but with so many different server types at the moment, and far too many ways to fix it. So search for

> *"Windows 2??? server fix certificate error"* (Note change *2???* To your server type) and follow the instructions you find. You will then never see this error again.

    c.   Ok we lied there is a third option. Close the browser and call a consultant to help you.

(TREND MICRO) | Worry-Free™ Business Security

LOG ON

Please type your password to access the product console.

Password: [   ] ▸ Log on

Forget your password? ⓘ

Install Security Agent

Click here to start installing the Security Agent to your computer.

Installing the client usually takes only a few minutes.

Copyright © 2003-2012. Trend Micro Incorporated. All rights reserved.

---

1. Now you can log into the console.

2. Now you will receive the second active request at the top of your browser asking you to run the console ActiveX DLL from Trend Micro.

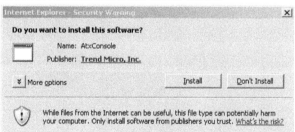

3. This must also be done for each computer accessing the web console. If by chance you are using a server that is 'too locked down', you will need to figure out how to allow for the install of ActiveX on that server before proceeding. Note lots of Windows servers are shipped 'too locked down' for ActiveX. A good search to use to fix the problem *is "Install ActiveX on IE Server 2???".*

4. You have completed installation of the WFBS console. You will now need to continue on with Agent installs and possibly the Exchange MSA install section. If you have completed all of those, move along to the administration part of the book for a look at the console itself.

Thoughts after installation:

- Make sure you have installed any Service Packs if they come out after this writing. Find them at *www.trendmicro.com/download*
- Update the security server and set up a schedule to get your updates (every hour please).
- Turn on and configure Antivirus and Anti-spyware.
- Do you have laptop users? Set up location awareness and roaming mode.
- Think about turning on and configuring Web Reputation, URL filtering and Behavior Monitoring.
- Set up a scheduled scan schedule.
- Set up notifications (you're not going to want them all).
- Install a few clients, make sure it works well and then install all your clients.
- Think you're done with the installs? Run TMVS to make sure.
- Setup your MSA (Exchange) anti-spam, content filtering and attachment blocking.
- Check your disk space; make sure you have lots of extra space.
- After a few days, check your server utilization; make sure it isn't overloaded. If you haven't played with Smart Scanning, you can now determine if your server can handle turning it on or not.
- Backup your settings.

Chapter 2: Status and Installs

The first screen you will see when you enter WFBS is the Live Status page. This is designed to show you everything you need to know in one page. Let's take a look.

Live Status

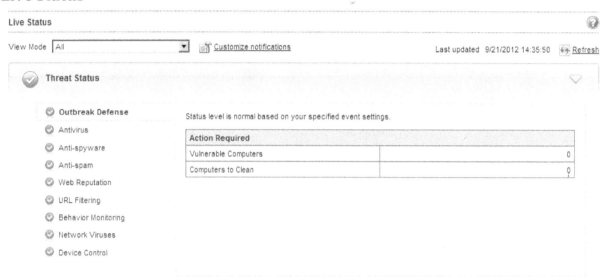

The top part of the screen will shows us a list of all the things WFBS is protecting us from. You will note the green checkmarks the first time you log in. This is good. As problems occur you will see these go from green to orange to red.

- **Green**: Everything is good or only very small problems exist
- **Orange**: You need to take action and deal with the computers listed.
- **Red**: A severe problem exists that must be dealt with immediately

Roll your mouse over each type of threat to see a list (or number of occurrences) appearing to the right. Clicking on the workstation name or incident number will let you drill down and find out more information on what happened.

What do the different statuses mean for each alert?

- **Antivirus**: It takes five viruses being found before the icon changes from green.
- **Anti-Spyware**: Again, five incidents will change the color from green.
- **URL Filtering**: This will alert from green after your users attempt to go to 300 websites you have disabled in URL filtering.
- **Behavior Monitoring**: Will list any behavior policies you have turned on
- **Network Viruses**: Viruses found by the WFBS Agent Firewall.
- **Outbreak Defense**: If an outbreak has been turned on, you will see information about it here.
- **Anti-spam**: Your MSA will update this every hour. You can click on the different levels (Low, Medium and High) to see the settings on your MSA.

- **Web Reputation**: Users will trigger this alert if they have gone to 200 sites listed in the Trend Micro Web Reputation database.
- **Device Control**: This will be triggered when you users try to use a device incorrectly according to your device control configuration.

- **Component Updates**: When you get updates (pattern files, small program changes….) Your server will tell its Agents that they need to download and install the updates. This section tells you how many Agents have not made those updates (they are now out-dated). Clicking on the number will give you a list of which Agents have the problem. You can hit the deploy now button to push another message to the Agents to update.
- **Update Now**: If your server has not done its updates in over 72 hours an alert will show up here and explain to you how long it has been since your last update. If you ever see this you need to hop on that 'Update Now' Button right away and then figure out what's wrong with your updates. If this update fails you will really need to figure out what's wrong before proceeding anywhere else.
- **Smart Scan**: Any Agents that have been disconected from the smart scan server .
- **Unusual System Events**: The WFBS Agent will report back any Disk Space problems on your servers.

- **License**: This will alert when you have either used up all your licenses (WFBS does count each install), or your license is about to expire (or has expired). When you license expires you will no longer get pattern files and program updates from Trend Micro.

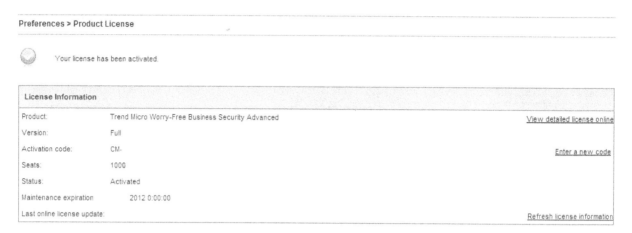

Clicking on 'Product License' will allow you to:

- **View Detailed License Online:** This will send you to the Trend Micro licensing website.
- **Enter New Code**: You can enter a new license code if you receive one (this is also how you would upgrade from evaluation to full version).
- **Refresh License Information**: When you renew your license you will be required to come here and click on the *'Refresh License Information'* link.

Installing Agents on your Workstations and Servers

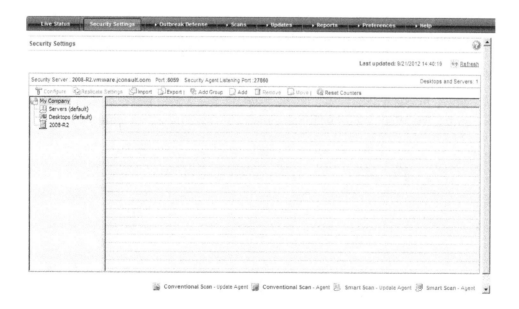

Dale Johnson

Here we will see how to install the Agents on our workstations and servers. The act of installation is simple.

1. We send a message (using the methods below) to the machine we want to install the agent on.
2. The workstation receives that message and downloads the product from the server.
3. It then installs the product.
4. After installation it contacts the server, and asks for the latest configuration and pattern files.
5. It downloads the files
6. Finally it goes into real time mode, listening for changes to your system to check for problems.

Add Button 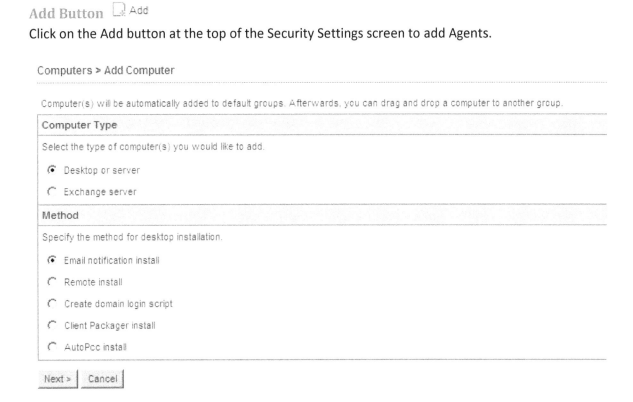 Add

Click on the Add button at the top of the Security Settings screen to add Agents.

Computers > Add Computer

Computer(s) will be automatically added to default groups. Afterwards, you can drag and drop a computer to another group.

Computer Type

Select the type of computer(s) you would like to add.

◉ Desktop or server

○ Exchange server

Method

Specify the method for desktop installation.

◉ Email notification install

○ Remote install

○ Create domain login script

○ Client Packager install

○ AutoPcc install

Next >   Cancel

Computer Type:

1. Desktop or Server: Selecting this means you will install the WFBS Agent to a Desktop (Workstation) or server.
2. Exchange Server: Selecting this means you will install the WFBS MSA on an Exchange server.

Email Notification

Email notification only works with the Workstation/Server Agent. WFBS will create an email, with a link back to the installer on the server that allows the user to click on the link to install program.

- NOTE: You must run this option from a computer that has email installed. It will use your email client to send the message

You can change the Email Subject to say whatever you like. Then add users email addresses of the user you want to send the message to. The program will open your email client and create an email message which you can edit and send to your users.

An Example of the text message you can change:

Please click on the URL link below. It will redirect to Trend Micro Security Server web page where you can download and install the Client/Server Security Agent.
https://192.168.0.1:4343/SMB/console/html/client/

- NOTE. The link will go back to the HOST name or IP address you choose during install. If the user can't see that HOST or IP, they will not be able to click on the link to do the install, unless you make changes to the email address. You will need to change the link to use the correct information they can connect with. An example of this is a laptop or home computer not in your network, maybe they can use the outside IP address of the server. VPN users can usually use this option when they are logged into your network.

AutoPCC

AutoPCC is simply the executable that allows you to install the Agent from the server. The executable is available online via the shared directory. You can access it with this link:

\\Server_Name\ofscan\AutoPcc.exe

This option will run the Remote Installer program, which will install the Agent on a workstation or a server visible on your network. To do this you must have the administrator rights (or the account information with those rights) on the machine you are installing on.

Note: You cannot use the Remote install program to install the Agent on the server WFBS is already installed on. You must install it by hand (autopcc.exe).

We recommend only installing one client the first time you run this program. After making sure the install ran fine, then you can go ahead and select more (or all) of your computers. The computers will be installed one at a time (to decrease bandwidth and server utilization issues).

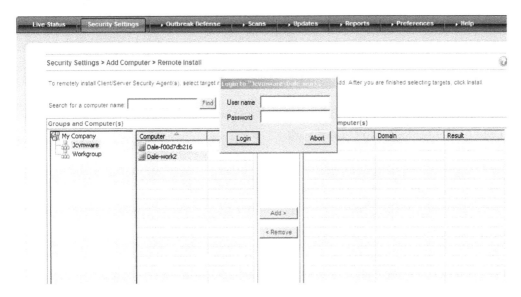

The screen will allow you to choose what workstations you want to install the WFBS Agent on. You can click on your domain names, find the computers you want to add, select 1 or more of them and hit the add button.

Once you click add a login screen will appear. Here you should put in your admin account information.

- If you have a domain: You will need to use your domain name in the login. So the username should look like:

    InsideWFBS8\administrator

- If you use a workgroup: You will need to use the local administrator to each workstation you are installing on. This means first you will need to add 1 machine at a time, and the username should look like:

    Workstation_name\administrator_name

You can also find the workstation\server by using the search option. Depending on your network you should be able to search via computer name or IP address.

A few gotchas:

- If the machine you are selecting is not online it will not be added to the list on the right side. If you type in the wrong administrator name and password, you will be kicked back and have to select the add button again.
- XP and Vista can have problems with the Windows firewall blocking the login. If you have problems take a look at turning off the firewall on those machines.

Once you have your workstation/servers listed on the right side you can click the Install button (hiding at the bottom). One by one your machines will start the install process.

Create Domain Login Script

If you use a domain, we will place the install script into a user's Login script. The install process will then run when the user logs into the network.

- If your users stay logged in overnight or for long amounts of time, then you will have to wait until they reboot or re-login to their machine to install.
- The script must have administrative rights on the computer when they login. In most cases this is true.
- The login script will work on the workstation that the user logs into. So, if you are going to do an install by hand on all your computers and you have administration rights, you will have to install the script on your user login, walk around and login to all the machines. Each will get the program installed.
- The user WILL SEE the install happen when they log into the domain. You might want to warn them if they are not used to things being installed without them knowing.
- The login script will keep the OFSCAN.BAT file in the users profile until you delete it from profile.
- It is recommended not to use this option on your servers.

Once you make this selection you will be given a help screen that simply sends you to run a program by hand to create the login script. That program is

Program Files\Security Server\PCCSRV\Admin\SetupUsr.exe

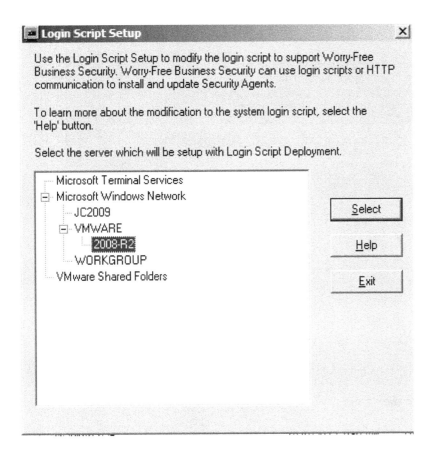

From the window find the domain and server that you want to add the login script to. You would usually select your domain controller here.

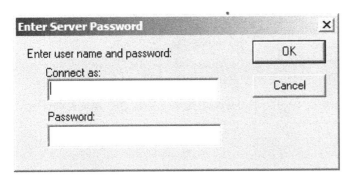

Type in the username and password to your domain using your domain name in the username like:

Insidewfbs80\administrator

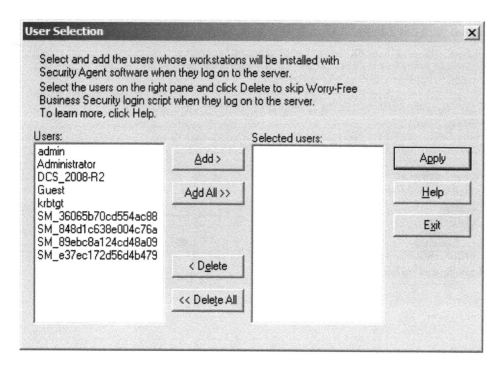

Select all of the users you want to add the login script to. Click on the Apply button and the script will be added to their login.

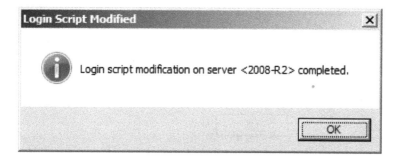

If you were to take a look at the user's profile you would notice that OFSCAN.BAT is now added to their login script:

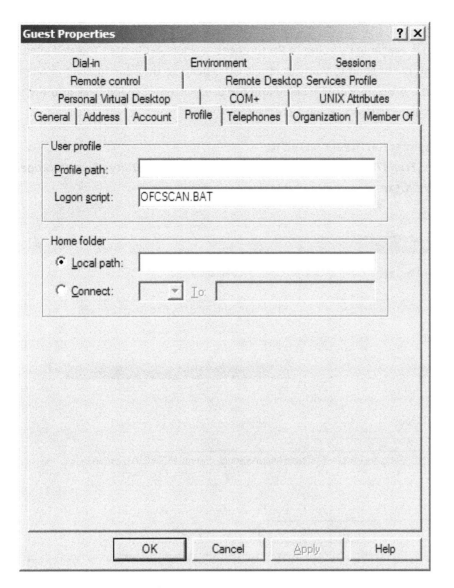

The OFCSCAN.BAT file can be found in C:\WINDOWS\sysvol\domain\scripts on your domain controller. It should simply contain the command to run AutoPCC

\\SERVER_NAME\OFCSCAN\AUTOPCC

This option (not listed) is available by going to Preferences -> Tools -> Clients. This will allow you to create an actual executable to send to your users (via CD is best) so they can install the Agent straight to workstation.   After they are installed and the users attempt to log back into the server, they will get any particular settings you have created for them.

- In windows explorer (on the server) go to
  Program Files\Trend Micro\Security Server\ PCCSRV\Admin\Utility\ClientPackager
  and run ***CLNPACK.exe***.

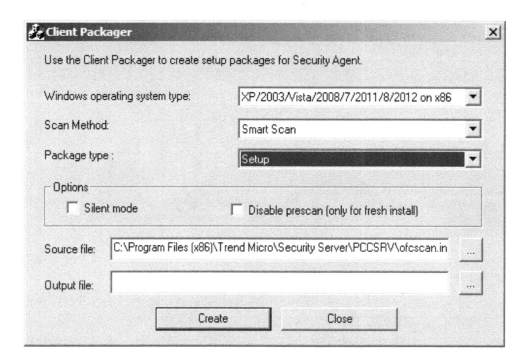

- **Target Operating System:**   Here you need to select information about the client you will be installing the agent on. First, is the workstation a 32 bit (x86) or 64 bit (x64)?
- **Package Type:** Are you installing the Agent as a new agent or updating from an old agent? It is recommend that if you are trying to upgrade old clients that you also create a new installation .exe along with your upgrade. If the upgrade fails the user will have to uninstall the Agent and reinstall it. You might as well get a step ahead and have it there with them to save you the headache when you get that phone call.
- **Scan Method:** You can choose Conventional Scanning or Smart Scanning option for the workstation.   You must have the Smart Scanning option enabled on your server to have the option on your workstations. For more information on the difference see Chapter 7.
- **Options:**
  - **Silent Mode:** The install is quiet and hidden from the user. The problem is, you went through all this only to have the user clicking on an .exe to start it. You might as well let them see something. If you want to hide it, hide it.

- **Disable Prescan:** Can only be chosen when you are installing the Agent as a new install. The option really makes no sense to choose unless you really have a short amount of time to do the install (or talk the user through it). It's always best to scan a workstation before installing an Agent.

- **Source File:**

  This is very important if you want to have the Agent you are installing connect to the server on a different IP address (like from the Internet). If you have various IP or host name options you can create an .ini file for each. The quick way of making a change is to:

  - Make a copy of the OFCSCAN.INI in your server directory.
  - Find the *"**Master_DomainName=**"* in the ini file. This should contain the IP address or domain name of your server. You can change this to the IP address or HOST name which your users will connect to your server with.

- **Output File:** Select a directory and name in which to store your outputted EXE file. The size of the output should be about 105-125MB.

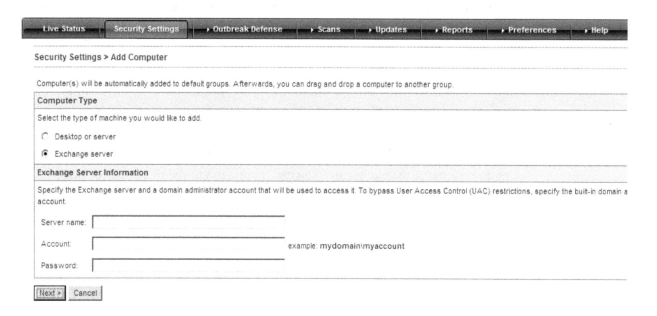

- Type in your server name. To find that name, go to the server that has your exchange loaded. *Right click on My computer -> Properties-> Computer Name*. The Server name is listed after ***Full computer name***:

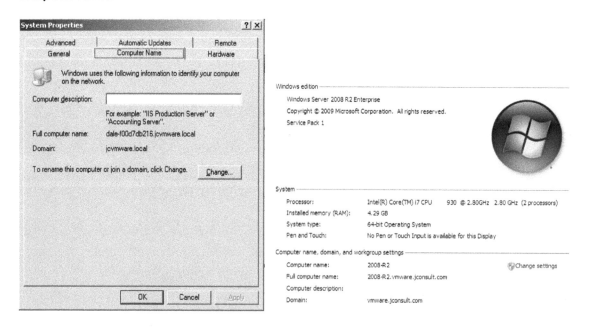

In my example the name is

2008-R2.insidewfbs08.jconsult.com

Hint: you can highlight the name and copy it from this screen to the installer screen.

- Account/Password: You will need the account used as the Exchange administrator. You will also need to use the domain in the username like:

  Insidewfbs80\administrator

- Once you hit next the program will first check the login rights of the server, along with making sure you have the correct Service Packs on both the server and the Exchange sever.

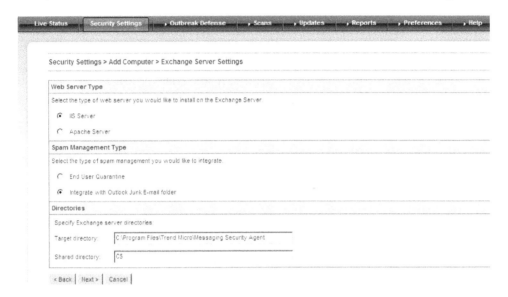

- **Web Server Type:** We again have to make to make a decision if we want to use the IIS or Apache server that is installed on the machine. This is (like with WFBS) to utilize the web console for administering the program. The web servers will need to be already installed.

- **Spam Management type:** Here we select how we want our Spam management to look from the users view.
  - **End User Quarantine:** This will create a separate folder in each users Outlook profile. All spam messages found as "iffy" will be sent to that folder. This is only an option if you are using Exchange 2003. Exchange 2007 will combine these messages automatically in the Junk folder.
  - **Integrate with Outlook Junk E-Mail Folder:** This selection will place all "iffy" mail into the current Outlook Junk Mail folder along with Microsoft's chosen spam messages. In Exchange 2003 this is an option. In Exchange 2007, everything will go to this folder anyways.
    - If you select the Junk E-Mail folder you must make sure you have already installed the Intelligent Message Filter on the server (Exchange 2003) or the Content Filter Agent (Exchange 2007)

- **Directories:**
  - Where would you like the MSA programs located? Note that you will be by default placing all the output (quarantines and log files) in this directory, so make sure it has room to grow.
  - **Shared Directory** to place the installation. If you're installing on the C:\ drive select C$...

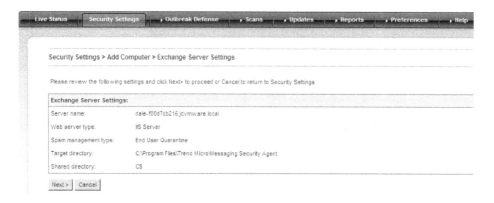

Here is a chance to review your selections. To go back and change, you will not have a back button, so but you must use the browser's back arrow. (I didn't write it, I just report it). Be careful, give it time; don't double click backwards.

BE CAREFUL!!!!   Once you select Next here you will start the install. There is no going back once you have started it!

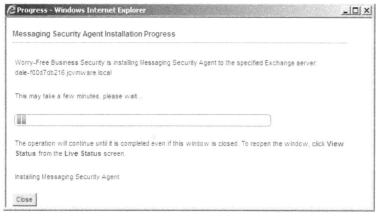

Update released

Trend Micro™ Worry-Free™ Business Security is now available. Upgrade to this version by following the link: Download.

St arting in WFBS 8 if there is a new version available of WFBS you will be notified and asked to download it. Now like every piece of software you have, being the first to download and try it, is probably not the smartest of moves. We recommend leaving that notice sit there for a bit of time, a week or three, and then doing the upgrade.

Turning off Agent downloads.

By default any Agent changes will automatically be sent downstream to your Agents the next time they connect to the server. This is fine and usually in an upgrade not a problem. BUT if you have network issues you will want to consider turning this option off and doing the upgrades later by hand.

If you want to turn off upgrades and handle them by hand in the console , you can go into Security Settings -> Workstations -> Agent Configuration -> Client Privileges -> Update Settings

Update Privileges

☑ Allow users to perform manual Update

☑ Use Trend Micro ActiveUpdate as a secondary update source

☐ Disable Security Agent upgrade and hot fix deployment.

(Check this box to disable the Security Agent upgrade. Pattern and engine updates will still be applied. Clear this box to keep all components up to date.)

- **Disable program upgrade and hot fix deployment**: This will stop all upgrade from going from the server down to the client. Turning this back on will then send the updates to all the computers in the system.

Upgrading

Once you click on the Download button the downloader program will be downloaded. It will tend to be called something like. WFBS_80_EN_ Downloader_Buildnumber.exe. This program should start by itself and ask you to then download the actual program. (Yes we know what you're thinking).

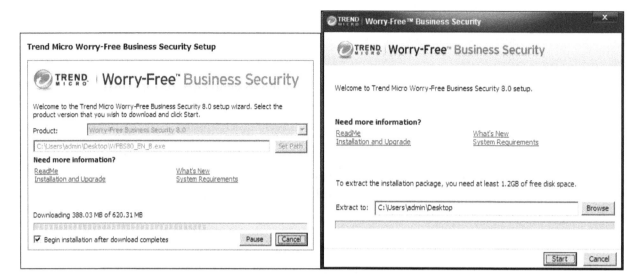

- If you left the '*Begin Installation after download completes*' checked off the download will start as soon as the file is downloaded. Or you will have to chase and start the upgrade yourself.
- Next we will be reminded that both a busy server will take a while and the WFBS services will be turned off to do the upgrade. If this is a problem click No and find a better time to do the upgrade.

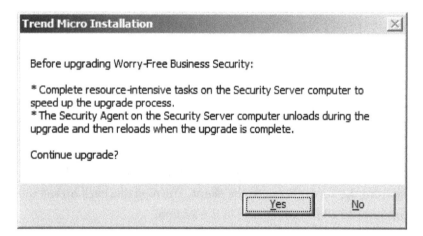

- The system will now check the WFBS Server to make sure everything is fine.

Dale Johnson

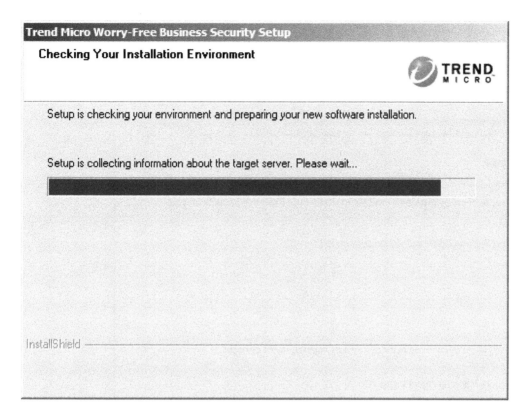

- Next if you have the WFBS MSA (Messaging Security Agent) installed the upgrade will ask you for a username and password that allows you to work inside Exchange. The Exchange admin is best here.

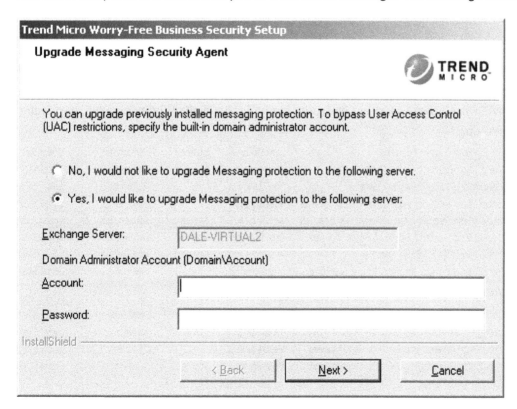

- The next few screens will install the WFBS Server, Check on the WFBS MSA setup and install those upgrades. An Upgrade to the Exchange Server is really an uninstall and reinstall of the software. So this will take some time to complete and your exchange server should bounce up and down twice during the upgrade.

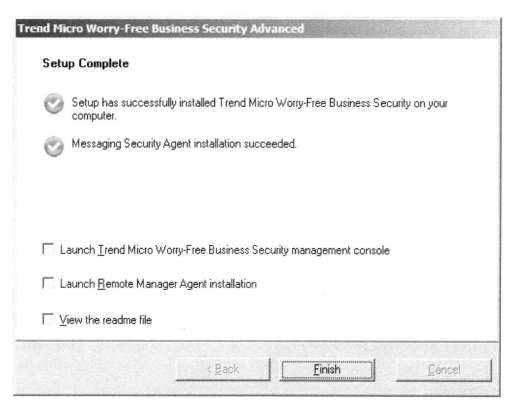

- Once the upgrade is complete you will be able to continue your work. But it is best to check and make sure your services are running. Those services are:
  - For WFBS itself these services. Note you might not have all of them installed, depending on your setup.

Trend Micro Plug-in Manager	Installs an...	Started	Automatic	Local System
Trend Micro Security (for Mac)	Manages t...	Started	Automatic	Local System
Trend Micro Security Agent Listener	Facilitates ...		Automatic	Local System
Trend Micro Security Agent NT Proxy Service	Scans net...		Manual	Local System
Trend Micro Security Agent RealTime Scan	Security A...	Started	Automatic	Local System
Trend Micro Security Server Master Service	Provides th...	Started	Automatic	Local System
Trend Micro Smart Scan Service	Provides s...	Started	Manual	Local System
Trend Micro Unauthorized Change Preventi...	Manages t...		Manual	Local System

  - For your WFBS MSA (Exchange). You should see all of these.

Trend Micro Messaging Security Agent EUQ ...	Messaging ...		Disabled	Local System
Trend Micro Messaging Security Agent Mast...	Messaging ...	Started	Automatic	Local System
Trend Micro Messaging Security Agent Rem...	Messaging ...		Disabled	Local System
Trend Micro Messaging Security Agent Syst...	Messaging ...	Started	Automatic	Local System

Dale Johnson

o   And finally make sure your Exchange Services are started. Depending on what Exchange you are using and your setup... you could have any combination of services. Make sure the ones listed as Automatic on your system are started.

Chapter 3 Agent Configuration

Security Settings

After installing the Agents, you can now make changes to the configuration of the whole group or each individual one. To do this, you must open up the Security Settings and look at your list of installed agents.

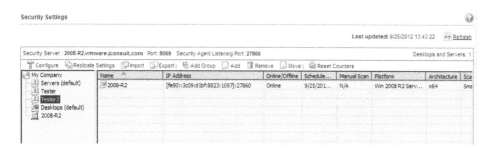

On the right hand side of your screen you will have listed Servers and Desktops under the My Company main section. If you have installed an Exchange Server that will be listed last in the list.

Agents

You can double click on each group to find a list of agents listed in the group. You will first notice that each Agent is marked Online or Offline. If you move the slider at the bottom of the screen to the right, you will also notice there are lots of stats on how each Agent is running and if it has found any problems. Included in the columns is what type of scanning method the Agent is using, Convention or Smart. Later in this chapter we will talk about these different scanning types.

Groups

The reason for groups is to divide your Agents into configuration groups, which simply means groups of Agents with the same configuration. Examples of good groups **are Laptops, Home Users, Servers** and **Desktops**. Each of these might (and probably will) have different settings. If you have smarter-than-average users that you trust you may consider a **Nerds** group. As we go through the settings we will use these groups to explain different reasons for choosing a confguration.

IMPORTANT: In this chapter, when you make configuration changes, you will either select a group or an individual agent. By selecting a group, the changes you make will go to EVERY machine in that group. By selecting an individual Agent you will only be sending the configuration to that one machine. If you make a change to one Agent in the group and then go to the top group to make a change, you will reset that change to all the Agents including that one you changed individually. The whole group will get the settings, including the individual Agent you had already changed. Be careful, and think about how to best use groups.

Add a New Group

Select the Add New Group button 🖺 Add Group from the top of the Agent screen.

Security Settings > Add Group

Group Type
Select the type of group you would like to add.
⊙ Desktops
⦿ Servers

Name
Specify a name for this new group.
Name: [   ]

Settings
You can import settings from an existing group to this new group and modify the settings later to suit your needs.
☑ Import settings from group: [Servers (default) ▼]

    Save | Cancel

- Group Type: Choose if your group will contain servers or desktops (workstations). You cannot combine servers and workstations in the same group.
- Name: Name the group
- Settings: If you have already created and configured a group that you want to replicate (at least most of) the settings from you can click in the import settings and select that group. The settings in a new group will take the program defaults.

Removing a Group

Simply click on the group you want to remove and click on the Remove button 🗑 Remove. The group will be removed. You cannot remove the default groups and you cannot remove a group that has Agents listed in it.

Moving an Agent

You can move an Agent between groups by selecting the agent you want to move. Drag and Drop it over another group in the same type. (I. E. servers into servers, desktops into desktops).

Removing an Agent

Security Settings > Remove Computer

Removal Type

Select a removal type below:

⦿ Remove the selected agent(s)

○ Uninstall the selected agent(s)

`Apply` `Cancel`

Once you have selected the Agent and hit the *Remove button* 🗑 Remove you will be asked if you want to:

- **Remove the Agent from the WFBS Server:** Once the client is removed the license will be updated with the correct agent count. If the client is still in use, the next time the client communicates with the server (in the next 180 minutes), they will reappear in the group and again take up the license count. This is best used for taking a computer that has been de-commissioned off of the server.
- **Remove the agent from the WFBS Server AND Uninstall the agent:** This will completely wipe the Agent off the workstation and remove it from the license count.

Moving your Settings

- Replicating your settings from one group to another is done like this: Select the Group you want to use for the settings. Click on the Replicate Settings button. 🗐 Replicate Settings

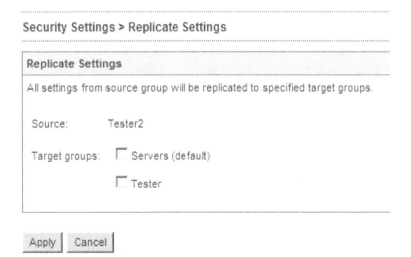

You will now have a list of like groups which you can transfer the settings to. Hit the apply button.

- ![Export] *Exporting Settings* is less useful in WFBS than it is in OfficeScan (its enterprise sister). But you can export the settings for the group into a file. Move the file over to another server and import it in. The file created is not editable, so it is not useful for making massive changes by hand (sorry).
- ![Import] *Importing Settings* from another server into the selected group.

Moving Agents to another Server

Security Settings > Move Desktop/Server

Move Desktop/Server

Move selected desktop(s) or server(s) on-line to another Security Server. Enter the new server name and port number below.

Server name: [   ]

Port: [8059]

Move   Cancel

If, by chance, you have more than one WFBS server you can utilize the Move button ![Move] Move to:

- Tell the Agent to change its settings to the other server
- The Agent will connect the other server
- The Agent will appear in that server's agent list
- And the Agent will download that server's Settings

This is useful if you are upgrading servers and decided to make the new WFBS on a different server.

Configuring the Agents

Now, let's go through the whole selection of options you have to setup each of your clients. I will also give you the default settings in case you go and do something crazy and need to come back to default.

First, select either a group or machine to configure by clicking on it to highlight it. Now select the Configure button ![Configure] Configure.

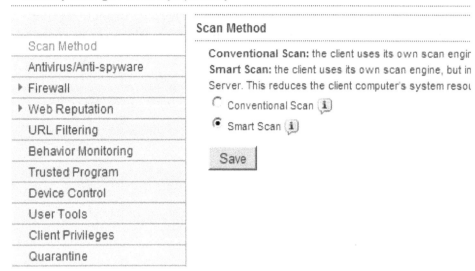

The first screen you see will have a left side where you can choose which part of the program to configure. Once you select each of those sections you will have a list of configuration files on the right.

NOTE: At the top of the screen you will see the option to turn on Smart Scan. This option is located in the Preferences section of the console and we will also talk about Smart Scan in that chapter.

Smart Scan

You can Enable or disable Smart Scan by Group.   To disable Smart Scan completely you must go to
Preferences -> Global Settings -> Desktop Settings -> General Scan Settings

- Smart Scan is a device that WFBS uses to help the Agents scan the workstations.   Your choices are to use either Smart Scan or a conventional scan.

  A conventional scan is when the Agent on the workstation scans files on its hard drives. As it scans the files it uses its own scan engine and pattern file to make decisions on what is considered an infected file.

  The Smart Scan takes scanning the next level and utilizes the server in scanning. As the program comes upon a file that has either been changed or is a new file, the Agent sends the server the information and the server will actually scan the file. If the Agent is not on the network or the WFBS server is not working, the agent will ask the Trend Micro Smart Scan Server (over the Internet) for a scan of the file.   If that fails, it will fall back on conventional scanning.

  Why is Smart Scanning used instead of just giving all clients the same data and ability to scan? Well, that is an interesting question. The big reasons are network utilization, install size, and a further level of security.   The data kept on the server is updated much more often and contains a different set of scanning tools.   To update this information with all the clients would be heavy on your network utilization.   Along with that, the install size of the Agent would become huge with all the information coming in about new files. Trend Micro has always worked hard at making the Agent a small footprint on your hard drive.   Finally, the Smart Scan can be used as a further level of scanning security for your Agents.   If by chance your agent becomes hacked or taken over by a Trojan, utilizing an outside scanner will allow for the WFBS server to take control of your workstation again.

We recommend waiting until your installation has been installed a week or so and then determining if your server can handle the extra hit that Smart Scanning will give it. The only reason you would turn it off is because you were seeing server utilization or network traffic issues.

Antivirus/Anti-Spyware

First, you should always have the *Enable real-time Antivirus/Anti-spyware* option checked. This allows the servers and workstations to look at files as they move or are opened on them. This is very important; turning this off will eliminate 95% of what WFBS is here to do. This will be turned on by default.

We are being asked what files you should scan. Now the first thing you're going to say is, "Why don't I scan everything all the time?" Well, even though that does seem smart, there are occasions and reasons to be a bit pickier about what we scan.

- **All Scannable Files.** Simply put, if it can be scanned (it's not encrypted in some way) we will scan it, every time it moves, is opened, is saved. Everything all the time.
- **IntelliScan.** Instead of looking at the file extensions (.bat, .exe, .doc….)while scanning, we will look inside the file header to figure out what it the file really is. This is set as the Default setting and unless you have a reason should remain so.

> *Inside IntelliScan*
>
> *Not every file is as it seems. Every file has an extension. This enables Windows to determine what program should run the program. .doc files are for a word processor. .exe files are executables. But anyone can change these extensions and therefore break how Windows starts a program. How/Why? Maybe you have worked for a company that didn't let you email pictures. To get around it you could simply rename the file from .jpg to .abc. The email system is only looking for picture file extension .jpg. Since .abc isn't blocked it lets the file go. In the email you tell the person on the other end to change the extension back to .jpg to use it. IntelliScan looks inside of every file it scans for the header, which tells WFBS more about the file then just what extension it has. In the header you will see stuff like what kind of file it is, when it was created, how big it should be…. IntelliScan allows you to stop your users from breaking the system by changing extensions, and more importantly, stops hackers from hiding bad programs behind the mask of a simple and boring file extension.*

- **Scan files with the following extensions**. Here we will look at only the file extensions to determine if a file should be virus checked. If you select this option you can edit the data inside the box to add or subtract extensions. We do not recommend this option unless you really, really have a good reason. After you think you have a good reason, you should then call someone to talk you out of it.

At what point should we scan a file?

- **Scan files being created, modified, or retrieved.** Set by default, this is by far the best option to choose. Why?
  - **Creating a file**: Any process can create a file on your computer. You don't see all the processes running on your computer unless you look. Check them out yourself if you like. *Ctrl-Alt-Delete ->Task Manager -> Processes*. There is a list of every process your machine is running. Each of these has the right to make a file. How do you know if a

hacker breaks into a program, and tells the program to start writing files (with a virus) to your computer? You don't. So check every file created on your computer.

- o **Modify a file**: Almost the same as creating a file, any process on your computer can open, modify and save a file. Many spyware programs are known to take good current files and turn them into virus seeds. This should also be checked all the time.
- o **Retrieving a file**: Ok, so we have the files on our computer taken care of, but what happens if you get a file from a server, or your email, or the Internet? These files must be scanned while we retrieve them before we put them on our computer.

Exclusions:

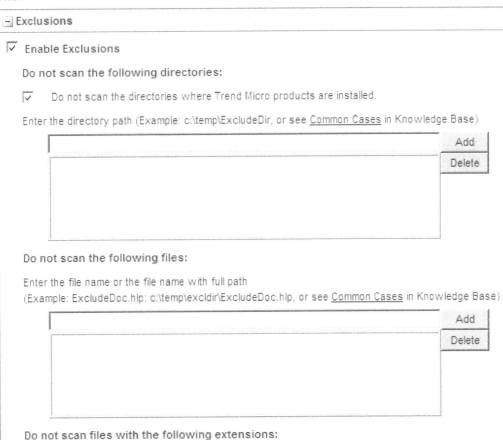

Directories: Not everything on the computer needs to be checked. Some things are a waste of time. A good example on a server is an Exchange or SQL Database. They are encrypted and scanning them will do nothing. WFBS allows us to either exclude files or whole directories. You should be careful about directories and ONLY exclude them on servers. One would hope that your server has good permissions set up so only specific processes can write to specific directories (Exchange is the only process that can write to the Exchange database directory).

File Names: There are also files you won't want scanned. Windows has a few that you might consider, but overall scanning them won't hurt anything and WFBS has a list of windows files it already knows to ignore. So what you should be interested here is if WFBS does anything funky with a homemade program you run on some or all of your workstations. The best example I have seen over the years is either your human resources or your accounting programs. These programs are notorious for doing funky things with databases and how they run on your computer. If you have these problems determined by yourself or with Trends Micro's help, you can put them in here.

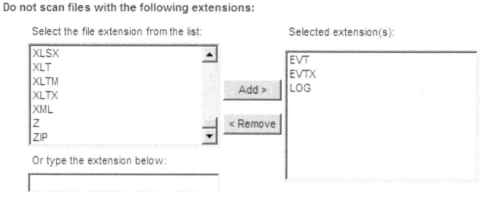

File Extensions: Excluding file extensions is a bit more dangerous. Here, you would be over-writing the IntelliScan option you set above by saying never scan any file with the following extension, even if it is another program hiding as this extension. Again if you find a program or file type that is being a problem, put it in here, but don't do that unless you are sure that it is the problem.

Advanced Settings:

Here we will look at a couple of options to help with the speed of virus checking.

Advanced Settings

For Antivirus Only

☐ Scan POP3 Messages

☐ Scan mapped drives and shared folders on the network

☐ Scan floppy drive system shutdown

☑ Enable IntelliTrap ⓘ

☑ Scan compressed files: up to 2 ▼ layers of compression

For Anti-spyware Only

Add certain types of Spyware/Grayware applications or files to the approved list to exclude them from scanning. This applies to all types of scans.

Modify Spyware/Grayware Approved List

- **Scan POP3 Messages:** Will work on all POP3 connections using Port 110. It will not work with SSL-POP3 (Exchange 2007). It will also not work with IMAP. A list of possible POP3 mailboxes to scan:
  1. Outlook 2000, 2002, 2003, and 2007 (not with Exchange 2007)
  2. Vista Windows Mail
  3. XP Outlook Express 6.0 with SP2
  4. Mozilla T-bird 1.5 and 2.0

  Because Pop3 only scans port 110 this pretty much leaves some of the major internet mail systems off the list. Gmail, for example, uses port 995.

- **Scan Mapped Drives and Shared Folders on your network:** Set to off by default, this will create both a good deal of network traffic and speed problems on your workstations if turned on. As long as all your workstations and servers have antivirus protection, there is no need for each individual workstation to check the files across the network.

- **Scan Floppy Drive System Shutdown.** In the olden days, we used to use these things called floppy drives. We would actually boot our computer using a floppy drive because we didn't have those newfangled 20MB hard drives that just came on the market. Because we would boot on the floppy, we would always check the floppy for a virus when we were shutting down the computer. Sort of a pre-boot check for the next time we turned the computer on. If you're not booting your computers on floppies anymore (and I hope you're not), then there is no reason to use this option.

- **IntelliTrap.** One way of hiding a virus is to compress it numerous times into a file. This can be an effective hack because your antivirus software is set to ignore compressed files with over X number of compressions. This is set on by default.

  In less nerdy terms, if I take an exe program and compress it into a zip file, it really doesn't do anything but it does change the file extension to .zip and now the header is a .zip file. So the exe is hidden behind the zip file and can only be found if the zip is opened. WFBS will check inside the zip file and look at the exe file to virus-check it. But what if someone keeps zipping the zip file, say 14 times? If so, your computer looks at the zip file and sees:

.zip -> .zip -> .zip -> .zip -> .zip -> .zip -> .zip -> .zip -> .zip -> .zip -> .zip -> .zip -> .zip -> .zip -> .exe

  Some virus protection programs (this one included) will allow you to choose how many levels of that zip file (or any compressed file) to look into before giving up. If the .exe is hidden deep enough, the virus protection will give up!

  IntelliTrap allows the WFBS to look into the compressed file, look real deep (20 layers or so), and check to see if anything is hiding. Different compression programs have different rules about levels of compression. IntelliTrap has a database of compressions types and is better than you at trying to figure it out.

- **Scan Compressed Files up to *X* layers.** Ah, we talked about this just a minute ago. Now we have to consider how much computer time and utilization it takes to unzip a .zip file 20 times to find that exe file. It takes a lot. So here we are going to limit the layers of compression to check for normal compressed files that IntelliTrap has already OK'd or ignored because it doesn't see a problem. Want to move it up to 6 (the limit)? Go for it. Odds are you will never even see a zip file that layered, but if you do you might as well check it.

- **Modify Spyware/Grayware Approved List**
  Allows you to decide to allow known Spyware or Grayware pattern files to be ignored by WFBS for this group. You should only do this when you know there is a problem with a pattern file interacting with the software you currently use on your workstations.

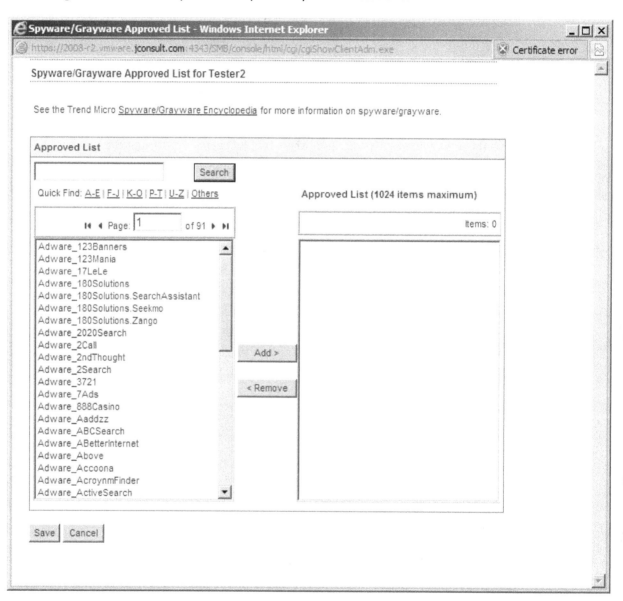

- **ActiveAction:** In the Actions tab, you will tell WFBS what to do when you encounter a problem. The default setting (Letting WFBS decide) is ActiveAction. In the last 10 years, viruses have become un-cleanable. Back in the 1990's viruses would try to infect a single file. Those files were sometimes cleanable, and you could actually use the file after cleaning the virus out of it. As virus writers have progressed, they no longer look into infecting single files, but have progressed into infecting your process DLLs and EXEs. So, Trend Micro has developed a system that determines by each infection type how to deal with the files infected. Some clients have found these settings to screw up their files and use the manual configuration noted below to setup their Agents. We recommend using Active Action if you're not sure about what options to choose and want to take the safe and simple option.

- **Customized Action:** If you want to configure your own, you will have a choice of what you want to do with the different types of infections. We recommend you Delete any Trojan, Spyware, or Packer. You should also either Quarantine or Delete the rest of the options (Generic, Virus, or Other). As we mentioned in the above paragraph, very little can be done to infected files, so either quarantining or outright deleting them seems the best.

```
─ Advanced Settings

☐   Display an alert message on the desktop or server when a virus/spyware is detected

    ☐   Display an alert message on the desktop or server when a probable virus/spyware is detected

☐   Run cleanup when probable virus/malware is detected
```

- **Advanced Settings:**
  - o **Display alert messages on desktop:** Do you want the users to know every time they have triggered a virus or spyware? This has its good points, keeping the users knowing when they are doing or when they are going to bad places. But it can be a Help Desk nightmare for some users. You might consider breaking your users up into two groups and having different options for each: Users I can deal with, and users I can't.
  - o **Display alert message for probable virus/spyware:** If by chance WFBS thinks it has found something wrong before it goes off and possibly cleans the problem it will alert the user that it has found something wrong and is going to try and fix it. You should probably only turn this on for users who actually understand what is happening.
  - o **Run cleanup when probable virus/spyware:** If the system finds that probable virus here it will go and try and fix it. It will ONLY do this if you choose ActiveAction and selected an action previously on this screen.

Firewall – In Office or Out of the Office

The Trend Micro Firewall is a Stateful firewall. This means it can block data by making rules and policies as it watches data. It can make these decisions based on current attacks or problems with the machine. The Firewall has been designed to select a different setting for in the office and out of the office. By default the Firewall is turned off, although the programming is installed with the Agent on each computer. We recommend that if you want to use the Firewall, you first set it up with one person in each group within your organization for at least a week. If no problems occur, you can then go forth in using the Firewall.

Firewall - In Office

Disabling the firewall will also disable Network Virus Protection and port blocking for Outbreak Prevention Policies (Outbreak Defense).

In Office Settings work as default settings if Location Awareness is disabled.
Review Location Awareness settings.

☐ Enable Firewall

  ⦿   Simple mode: Enables the firewall with Trend Micro default settings.

  ○   Advanced mode: Configure the security level, IDS, notifications, and exceptions.

[Save]

Simple Mode: The default settings will allow all inbound and outbound traffic while blocking ports that are utilized by network viruses. It will specifically always allow ports 21, 23, 25, 53, 80, 110, 137, 138, 139, 443, 445, 16372, 16373 to flow traffic.

Advanced mode: Will allow you to make customized settings for your machines.

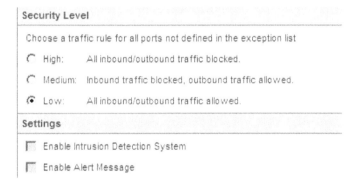

Security Level: Here you can choose what you want to allow in and out of the machines. You would only change this if you were having an outbreak problem in your network. This can be very dangerous and overrides every port on your system.

  High: Turn everything off, no communication except for the Agent itself talking to the server. The only traffic that travels is through any ports you placed in your exception list. It is equal to just turning your computers off as in most organizations, this will eliminate the workstation talking to Active Directory and other communications to do their daily work.

  Medium: This will turn off any inbound traffic. The only traffic that travels is through any ports you placed in your exception list. The user will have to start a conversation with an open port for data to be retrieved.

Low: allow all inbound and outbound traffic while blocking ports that are utilized by network viruses. Low is selected by default.

Intrusion Detection System: A smart method of finding attacks to your machine. When turned on, IDS will attempt to find different intrusions before they get into your machine. We recommend using this if you do not have a Firewall on your network that already does IDS. If you use a Firewall, these options really won't be necessary. Intrusions detected include:

- SYN Flooding
- Conflicting ARP
- Oversized Fragments
- Ping o' Death
- Overlapping Fragment
- Teardrop Attack
- Tiny Fragment Attack
- Fragmented IGMP
- LAND Attack

If Trend Micro finds a new Intrusion that needs to be caught, they will possibly make an update in the future to add more intrusions to the list. This Intrusion list has been pretty static over the last several years.

Enable Alert Message: Do you want the users to know different ports are now being blocked or an intrusion has been detected trying to get on their machine?

Enable Certified Safe Software Service: This is another level of protection that allows the Client to query the Trend Micro servers for information about Malware Blocking. This is an excellent option to enable if you have the bandwidth to handle it.

- **Local:** Enable the local Certified list downloaded routinely with the other pattern files
- **Global:** Enable the Client to contact Trend Micro for the latest update in the Trend Micro database.

Exceptions

Add or edit exception rules.

Add   Edit   Remove   Move Up   Move Down

	ID	Name	Action	Direction	Protocol	Port/Port Range	Machine
☐	1	DNS	Allow	Bi-directional	TCP/UDP	Specified 53	All
☐	2	NetBIOS	Allow	Bi-directional	TCP/UDP	Specified 137, ...	All
☐	3	HTTPS	Allow	Bi-directional	TCP	Specified 443	All
☐	4	HTTP	Allow	Bi-directional	TCP	Specified 80	All
☐	5	Telnet	Allow	Bi-directional	TCP	Specified 23	All
☐	6	SMTP	Allow	Bi-directional	TCP	Specified 25	All
☐	7	FTP	Allow	Bi-directional	TCP	Specified 21	All
☐	8	POP3	Allow	Bi-directional	TCP	Specified 110	All
☐	9	MSA	Allow	Bi-directional	TCP	Specified 16372, ...	All

Exceptions: A List of exceptions is given. In the Simple setting all of these are selected and allowed to communicate even if a network virus is found. You maybe want to consider not selecting FTP (Port 21), Telnet (Port 23) as most users have no need to utilize these protocols.

If you want to lock down the use of outside mail systems, you can also not allow SMTP/POP3 (ports 25 and 110) and actually setup a deny action using the Add button.

Creating your own Rules: You can create your own rules to set up a few scenarios like:

- Allow a user only to FTP inside the office
- Deny SMTP mail only to your internal mail server
- Allow only certain users to access the Internet

Click on the *Add Button* Add .

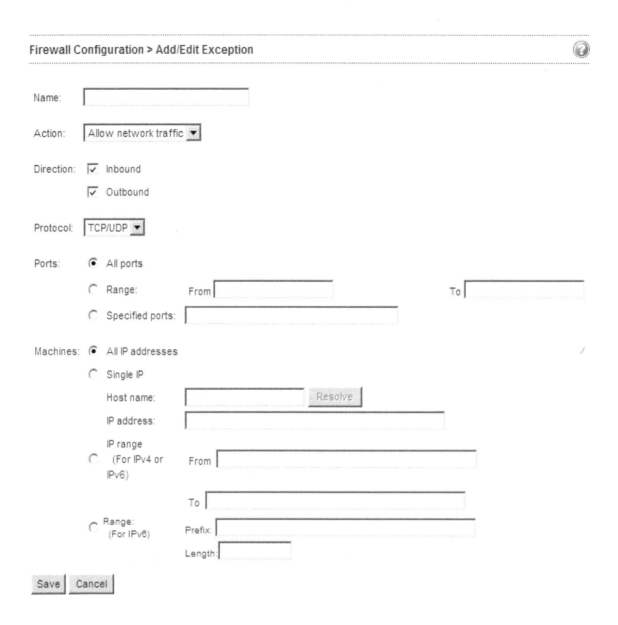

When you create a rule you will need to:

- Name your rule
- Choose Allow or Deny traffic
- Allow or Block inbound or outbound traffic
- Which protocol would you like to work with? TCPUDP, TCP, UDP, or ICMP
- Which ports using that protocol would you like to block?
- When blocking the traffic is there specific IP address(es) you would like to deny or allow traffic to; this can include a single IP or host name, a range of IPs or all IPs

Web Reputation

Like the firewall settings you can setup Web Reputation separately for in the office and out of the office. Web Reputation allows you to stop your users from going to known bad websites. These websites can have viruses, security risks, and or Trojans.

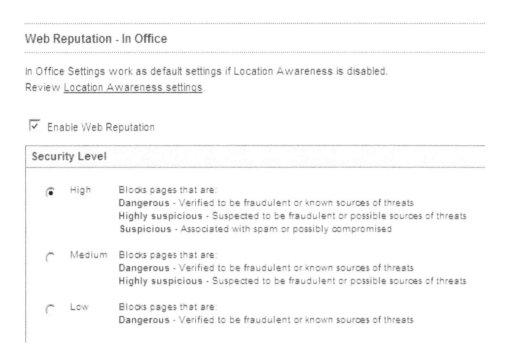

Trend Micro maintains a database of websites that it considers to have reputations (bad ones for this talk). They have divided those sites up for WFBS in the following categories:

- **Verified fraud pages or threat sources:** These are known web sites and pages that have a virus, spyware, or such attached to them. If you go there you will have a problem.
- **Suspected fraud pages or threat sources:** These sites have been found to have problems but have a lower rating as either the problems with the site aren't full time or some people consider the threat ok (like a screensaver program). It is probably best to try this setting and see if your users complain about not going to these sites.
- **Associated with spam or possibly compromised:** These sites are from known spammers or maybe have been compromised due to the web system they are running. Certain types of websites are less secure than others, these sites are in the very unsecure zone and either can be or have been compromised. Choosing this will block some sites your users might actually use. Sadly, lots of websites are ignored by their webmasters. They have been left alone or the webmasters don't care to secure them.
- **Unrated pages:** Mostly new pages that simply haven't been rated. A webpage needs to be searched or used by Trend Micro's clients and its internal servers before it gets a rating. I would probably not use this option for your users, the web grows so many pages a day that your users will come across new pages often enough to make this a bit annoying.

Can you see the pages listed in these groups? No. Trend Micro keeps the database secure so that the hackers that make these sites won't know that they have been found.   You can search individual web sites using their reclassification tool at: http://reclassify.wrs.trendmicro.com/ .   You can also tell Trend Micro about websites you either want to add to the database or sites you want them to take off the database. This webpage can only be used by administrators and will make you put in your license key to secure that only Trend Micro clients are doing updates.

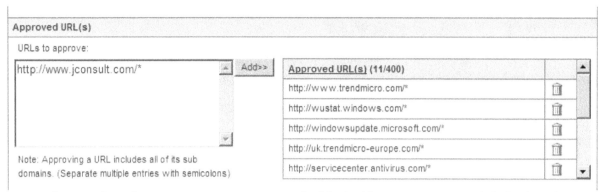

Approved URLs: If you have URLs you want never to be blocked by WFBS, you can include them her. You must use http:// (or https://) and a '*' to signify the whole website. Two examples are:

*http://www.jconsult.com/** - Will allow you to go to any page on jconsult.com.

http://.jconsult.com/**- Will allow you to go to any page on any subdomain of jconsult.com

URL Filtering

URL filtering is how you can stop your users from going to websites you don't want them to. You can choose to control these pages either during work hours or all the time.

URL Filtering

URL filtering screens Web pages using content categories on Trend Micro servers. To select specific types of Web sites to block during different tir of the day, select Custom and configure the table below

☑ Enable URL Filtering

Filter Strength	
○ High	Blocks known or potential security threats, inappropriate or possibly offensive content, content that can affect productivity or bandwidth, and unrated pages
○ Medium	Blocks known security threats and inappropriate content
● Low(Default)	Blocks known security threats
○ Custom	Select specific page categories to block

This is a bit redundant of Web Reputation and works in the same way. The difference between the two is that filtering is looking at the content of the webpage rather than what the webpage may do to you. So, a webpage listed on one bad list might not appear on another. We can make changes and configure the pages as we wish, but Trend Micro by default has built some basic levels we can choose from:

- **Block known security threats**: Trend Micro maintains a list of known bad web pages that if you go there, you will be attacked. This database is very much like its Web Reputation sister.
- **Inappropriate Content:** Trend Micro maintains a list of websites that most organizations would consider inappropriate. An example of those categories can be seen in the Filter Rules section. You can either turn this on, or use the custom setting and maintain the categories yourself.
- **Content that can affect productivity and bandwidth:** Sites that affect productivity tend to be social sites and community forums, while bandwidth-depleting sites will tend to be photographers' websites, software download sites, Internet radio and video sites.

- **Custom**: Customize the different categories to meet your organizational needs.

Filter Rules		
URL Category	☐ Business Hours	☐ Leisure Hours
+]Adult	☐	☐
+]Business	☐	☐
+]Communications and Search	☐	☐
+]General	☐	☐
+]Internet Security	☑	☐
+]Lifestyle	☐	☐
+]Network Bandwidth	☐	☐

You can click on each group and search down further into the different categories you want to choose.

Business Hours: We can also select what your users can do on off hours or during work hours.

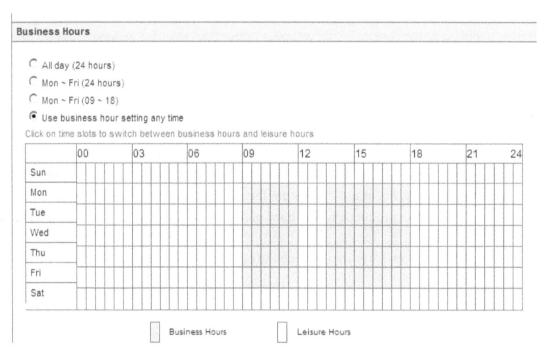

- **Business and Leisure hours** used to be popular when the Internet was just starting. This was a way for employers to let their users get time on the Internet on their off hours. As home connectivity has grown, users have relied less on the business Internet connection for their own personal use. But if you have users whom you would either like to learn to use the Internet more or if they don't have reliable connections at home, you can utilize this to give them a nice safe way of surfing the internet.

How much of the day would you consider business hours?

- **All Day**: Simple select the All Day (24 Hour) option and there will be no leisure time settings on your network.
- **From Morning to Night:** If you want your users to be able to be more open before and after work hours you can set:
  - Morning: From Starting Time To 12
  - Afternoon: From 12 to ending time

Manual Configuration: You can also click in the Week Graph to determine by hand which hours are considered Business and which are Leisure.

Want to give your users up to a two hour stretch at lunch?

- Morning: From Starting Time to 11 (for 11am to noon lunch) or 12 (for 12 to 1 lunch).
- Afternoon: 12 (for 11am to noon lunch) or 1 (for 12 to 1 lunch) to ending time.

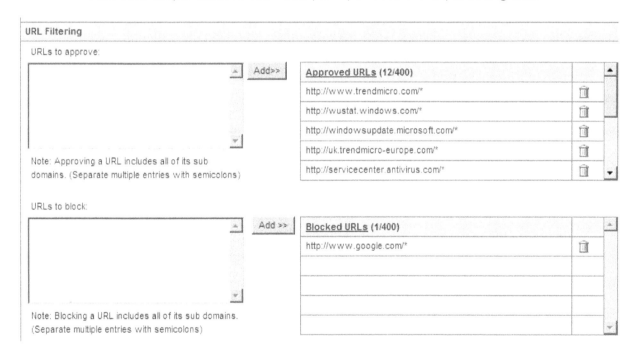

Approving and blocking URLs: WFBS allows you to add approved and blocked websites into the Web Reputation and URL Filtering parts of the Agent.   By default, all of the Trend Micro and Microsoft websites you will need to run and update your computer are already added.

You must use http:// (or https://) and a '*' to signify the whole website. Two examples are:

- *http://www.jconsult.com/*   - Will allow you to go to any page on jconsult.com.
- *http://*.jconsult.com/*- Will allow you to go to any page on any subdomain of jconsult.com

Behavior Monitoring

Behavior Monitoring enhances endpoint protection by proactively stopping unknown malware. It continuously watches for malicious program activities and blocks questionable programs.

☑ Enable Behavior Monitoring

☐ Enable Intuit QuickBooks Protection ⓘ

☑ Enable Malware Behavior Blocking ⓘ

One of the ways of watching for bad programs (and users) is to watch the files and settings they attempt to change. Sadly, Windows has lots of ways of attacking the operating systems (it's limitless). Some of them are old, some of them are new and some haven't even been thought of yet.

The basics behind behavior monitoring are to watch certain parts of your computer that can easily change what your computer is doing. We check what processes run on the computer and how (or where) you go when you view the internet. When WFBS sees a bad action happen, it will either block the action from happening, stop the process from happening, or alert the user its happening and let the user decide what to do (kind of scary).

- **Enable Intuit QuickBooks Protection:** If you use QuickBooks, this is a great option to turn on. It will check your QuickBooks data, so that it can only be changed or opened by the QuickBooks process itself.
- **Enable Malware Behavior Blocking**: Turning on this option will tell the agent to keep track of how the user works when opening shares, ports, and other network resources. WFBS will first determine the average network uses of the user. It will then (with this feature turned on) determine that something is going wrong and malware might be attacking the system if all of a sudden the user opens up three or four times the amount of shares at once, or starts transmitting over 10 new ports. These are not exactly the thresholds, but an example of how the system works.

Exceptions

Programs in the approved list are not monitored for suspicious behavior, while programs in the blocked list are automatically blocked.

Enter Program Full Path

Example: C:\Program Files\BMDir\BMSample.exe (Use semicolon to separate entries)

[Add to Approved List] [Add to Blocked List]

Approved Program List

Name	Program Full Path	

Blocked Program List

Name	Program Full Path	
calc.exe	C:\Windows\System32\calc.exe	🗑

Exceptions: Adding Approved and Blocked programs to WFBS

If you have a problem with either a known hack you want to block, or a good program (Like a HR or accounting system) you would like to be ignored by behavior monitoring, you can add them here.

You will need to place the full path and file name into the box at the top, and select either block or approve. You can place multiple programs at the same time by separating them by using a semi-colon (;) between each. Do not put them on separate lines as this will not work correctly.

Also, because you have to have the full path, blocking hacks is not usually very effective as the hacks change their directory and file names on pretty much every install of the product. But, if you know of something you are sure about, you just might be able to block it using the block exception.

Trusted Program

Trusted Program

Programs listed in the Trusted Program List will not be monitored for suspicious file access activities.

Enter Program Full Path

Type the full file path, using a specific file path.
<drive_name>:\<path>\<file_name>
Example: C:\Program Files\TrustDir\TrustSample.exe
(Use semicolon to separate entries. See Common Cases in Knowledge Base.)

Add to Trusted Program List

Trusted Program List

Name	Program Full Path	
cmd.exe	c:\Windows\System32\cmd.exe	🗑

WFBS will allow you to take any program on your systems or network and trust it. This means this trusted program will not trigger any WFBS Agent to think it is causing a problem. This is probably recommended for any in house programs you use or your accounting or HR systems. Also if a program is doing high amounts of Memory, Disk, or Network traffic you may consider putting it on the list so that all of its traffic is not monitored by the Agents.

Add to Trusted Program List: Find where you program is installed on around your network and type in all the possible locations of the program exe into the trusted list. Two Examples are:

c:\Windows\System32\cmd.exe

C:\Program Files (x86)\Trend Micro\Security Agent\IPXfer.exe

Device Control

Device Control allows you to secure what goes on or off of your Network Shares and USB Devices.

Device Control

Device Control regulates access to external storage devices and network resources connected to computers.

☑ Enable Device Control

   ☑ Enable USB Autorun Prevention

Device Type	Permissions
USB storage ⓘ	Full access ▼
Network drives ⓘ	List device content only ▼

- **Enable USB Autorun Protection**: Disables any program installed on a USB to automatically install on your computer. This is a trick used by many Trojans and Root kits to get on your computer without you knowing. It is highly recommend you leave this on. If there is a program to run on the USB, you can still run it by hand.
- **Permissions**: For each device (USB and Network Shares) we can chose how we want the user to access the data.

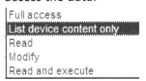

    - **Full Access**: Allows the user to Explore, Read, Write Execute, Delete or Change anything on the device.
    - **List device content only**: Will only allow the user to list out the top level files on this device. They will not be able to open or move any files.
    - **Read Only**: User will be able to Open and Copy any file from the device.
    - **Read and Write Only**: Allows the User to Open, Copy, Save or Delete any file from the device.
    - **Read and Execute Only**: User will be able to Open, Execute and Copy any file from the device.
- **USB Recommendations**. Usually good data is transferred between workstations with USBs. If anything we probably recommend *Read and Write Only Access*, as the average user shouldn't be trading executable files via USB. Do note: if you use a USB to move executables, you should place yourself in your own group and set this option to allow yourself to run them.
- **Network Resource Recommendations**: All of your network shares should be secured using Windows Security. That being said, opening shares between users usually lacks all kinds of

security. We then recommend either Read Only or Read and Execute Only access to secure infections from being transferred between workstations.

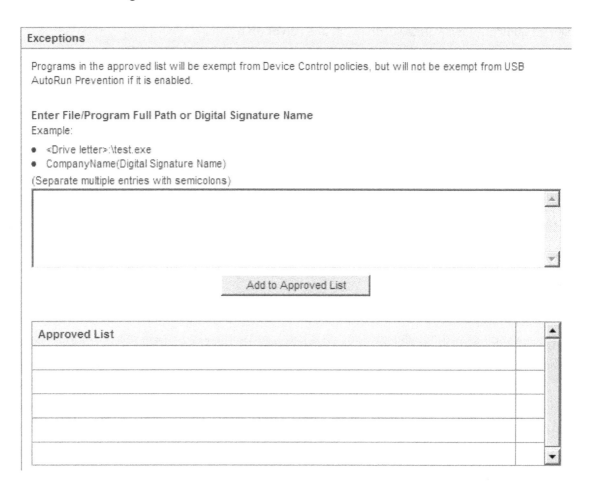

- **Exceptions**: If you routinely move certain files between USBs or Network Shares you can add them to the Exceptions List. Note if you enable the USB autorun option, you cannot make an exception to autorun a file on the USB.

Dale Johnson

User Tools

For Desktop users only. The following Tools are enabled by installing the Trend Toolbar (Which will be installed if one of these options is selected).

User Tools

The following end user tools provide additional security:

Wi-Fi Advisor

☐ Enable. Determines the safety of a wireless connection by checking the authenticity of access points based on the validity of their SSIDs, authentication methods, and encryption requirements.

Anti-Spam Toolbar

☐ Enable. Filters spam in Microsoft Outlook.

- **Wi-Fi Advisor :** Encrypts transactions on wireless connections. Also includes a wireless safety toolbar to show your users when they are on an unsecured wireless connection. This is very useful for your traveling laptop users.
- **Trend Micro Anti-Spam toolbar :** Working only with the following programs, this will enable users too quickly determine when a mail is spam message.
    - Outlook 2002, 2003, 2007
    - Outlook Express 6 SP2
    - Vista Windows Mail

Client Privileges

In the configuration privileges you will determine what the client can do via their Agent Console.   Trend Micro likes not to give the users many privileges; by default all of the options are turned off. The Agent chapter will talk about what the users see when you turn on these options.

Antivirus/Anti-spyware

☐ Real-time Scan settings   ☐ Manual Scan settings

☐ Scheduled Scan settings   ☐ Skip Scheduled Scan

Manual Scan Settings: Allows the users to set the settings when they manually scan their own computers. If you do not allow this option, they still will have the manual scan option, just won't be allowed to make changes to the settings (They won't see the option to make the changes). Overall we don't really see a problem with this option. If the user is smart enough to scan on their own in the first place, they should be smart enough to control how the scan works.

Scheduled Scan Options: Allows the users to change the frequency and time of the scans, what files to scan, and what to do during the scan. For the most part we don't recommend this option being set. If you have a group of users who you can trust not to disable the scheduled scan, maybe putting them in their own group and giving them the option might be ok. Overall, leave this option off.

Real-time Scan Settings: Allows the users to determine what files to scan (written, created, retrieved), the ability to turn off IntelliScan, what drives to scan, and what to do when they find a virus. This again is a dangerous option to give most users and should remain off.

Skip Scheduled Scan: Allowing the user to skip a scheduled scan as it happens. This is VERY, VERY dangerous, as 90% of users will stop a scan if they know they can. Leave this option off.

Firewall
☐ Firewall settings

Firewall Settings: If the firewall is turned on (in the firewall settings), the firewall option will appear in the Protection tab (yes there is no firewall tab). The user will then be able to enable/disable Intrusion Detection Systems (IDS), receive notification when a firewall action happens, and be able to look at their network cards and see the open ports and protocols that the firewall is watching. If you have users that can handle how IP works on their machines, they may find this option useful, but for the most part if you enable the firewall, you will not want to enable this option.

Web Reputation - Continue Browsing
☐ Will show a link that allows users to continue browsing a particular malicious URL until the computer is restarted. Warnings will still show on other malicious URLs.

Web Reputation: Allows the users to continue to the blocked page once the Web Page warning is displayed telling the user the website is a problem and should be skipped. We do not recommend turning this option UNLESS you really do trust your users not to ruin their systems and control where they go. Rebooting a workstation will cause the website message to reappear for the user, even if they have said they want to go to the website before.

URL Filtering - Continue Browsing
☐ Will show a link that allows users to continue browsing a particular restricted URL until the computer is restarted. Warnings will still show on other restricted URLs.

URL Filtering: Allows the users to continue to a page once the Web Page warning is displayed telling the user the website is restricted and should be skipped. We do not recommend turning this option. Why would you use URL blocking in the first place, if you are going to let them go there.

Behavior Monitoring

☐ Allow users to modify Behavior Monitor settings.

Behavior Monitoring: Under the Protection tab in the Agent; allows the users to turn Behavior Monitoring on or off, add to the exception list, and edit what QuickBooks files are under protection. Like many other settings, enabling this will allow your users to turn off the settings and shouldn't be selected for most users.

Trusted Program

☐ Allow users to modify Trusted Program list.

Trusted Program: Under the Protection tab in the Agent; allows the users to add a program to the exception list. Like many other settings, enabling this will allow your users to turn off the settings and shouldn't be selected for most users.

Proxy Settings

☑ Allow users to configure proxy settings

Proxy Settings: If proxy settings are enabled, this will allow users (under the Security Protection tab) to change or turn off the proxy server. Most users will not understand why they use a proxy server, and odds are you won't want anyone ever playing with these setting, so it would be best never to turn this on.

Update Privileges

☑ Allow users to perform manual Update

☑ Use Trend Micro ActiveUpdate as a secondary update source

☐ Disable Security Agent upgrade and hot fix deployment.

(Check this box to disable the Security Agent upgrade. Pattern and engine updates will still be applied. Clear this box to keep all components up to date.)

Allow users to perform manual Update: Allows the user to update their pattern files now. This is very useful for all users and a must for Roaming users. '*Update Now*' will appear by right clicking the Agent icon.

Use Trend Micro ActiveUpdate as a secondary source: Allows the Agent to get its update from Trend Micro directory if either the server is not available or they are not in a location to see the server. This was called Roaming Mode in previous versions of WFBS. This is very useful and should be used for laptop or home users.   Roaming users will attempt to connect to the server on the normal internal update schedule, connecting to the Trend Micro server if they do not make the connection. If a user connects to the Trend Micro servers, they will NOT receive configuration and profile updates until they connect again to the WFBS server. The exact connection order is:

1. Connect to server
2. Server times out, connect to Trend Micro
3. Check updates, if available download
4. Connection closes like normal.

Disable program upgrade and hot fix deployment: This should only be turned on when there are machines, which have the Agent installed, that must not have software changes to them unless they have been tested. We have seen this often on lab equipment. Turning this off means that a machine can fall way behind on their software running on it and become a risk.

Client Security: Will stop all programs and hacks from doing anything to the Agents file, directories and registry entries. This is very important to select and use on all users.

Quarantine

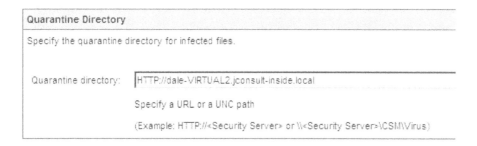

This will allow you to choose which WFBS server the users will send quarantined files to (if you have quarantining turned on). You should only change this option if you have more than one WFBS server on the same network.

Chapter 4 - Outbreak Defense and Vulnerability Scanning

Outbreak defense is how Trend Micro makes sure that your WFBS knows and reacts to a major world-wide attack. What happens is this: Trend Micro will see an outbreak of some attack over the internet. It will take the information from the attack and create a Threat Package. This package contains information on how to find the virus, what the virus does and how it communicates. They send the Threat Package down to all their clients who utilize Outbreak Defense and have it installed on their systems. The WFBS and Enterprise servers will then take the information, send it along to all the workstations and servers connected to them. Those machines will then know how to protect themselves from the outbreak.

The second set of information sent down from Trend Micro is the Cleanup Package. This is also sent to all its clients and explains to them the best way to clean any machines that were infected.

Once the threat has passed and Trend Micro sees the end of the attack, it sends a message to the user base turning off the Outbreak Defense, and includes the information it learned in the pattern files that are also updated.

What can be protected during an outbreak?

- Access to files (Writing to and creating files).
- Port blocking.
- Checking for vulnerabilities on your clients that are used by the attack.
- Blocking certain extensions and phrases in emails (Via the MSA Agent).
- Blocking file sharing

You can turn off an Outbreak Defense by clicking on the *Delete* button listed under *Automatic Response*.

During an Outbreak one of the three Buttons will show up in Yellow (the others in gray). This will explain what stage the outbreak is currently in.

Prevention

Threat Information					
Threat	Alert Type	Risk Level	Delivery Method	Vulnerability Exploited	Automatic Response
	N/A				Disable
Date/Time Initialed		Date/Time End		Automatic Response Details	
N/A		N/A		N/A	

During prevention the screen will show the name of the threat, level of the threat (which will always be red), and the type of threat. You will also be able to view how WFBS is responding to the threat by clicking the View button (under Automatic Response Details).

Alert Status for Online Computers		
Computer Type	Enabled	Not Enabled
Desktops/Servers	N/A	N/A
Exchange servers	N/A	N/A

A count of your total desktops/servers and Exchange server will appear. A list of machines that have not gotten the Outbreak policy will be listed. It would be a good thing to check that list and determine why they have not received the information.

Potential Threat

Vulnerable Computers: Shows all the computers that the last vulnerability assessment found with problems. They are ranked by their risk level and therefore the level at which you should worry about fixing the workstations.

- **Scan for Vulnerabilities Now**: Will scan the network to find computers that are at risk. This should be an operation you run normally when you feel something is wrong with your network.

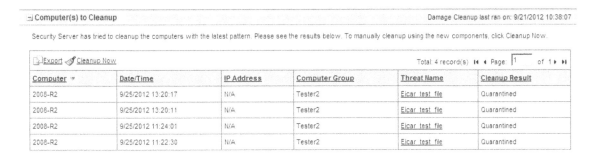

Computer ▾	Date/Time	IP Address	Computer Group	Threat Name	Cleanup Result
2008-R2	9/25/2012 13:20:17	N/A	Tester2	Eicar_test_file	Quarantined
2008-R2	9/25/2012 13:20:11	N/A	Tester2	Eicar_test_file	Quarantined
2008-R2	9/25/2012 11:24:01	N/A	Tester2	Eicar_test_file	Quarantined
2008-R2	9/25/2012 11:22:30	N/A	Tester2	Eicar_test_file	Quarantined

Computers to Cleanup: As the machines report back to the WFBS server, on their state, the server will build a list of machines that have been infected. You will be able to select some or all of the machines and click on the *Cleanup Now* button. The list will then update, explaining which machines have either failed clean up or are still in the process of being cleaned. If, after the cleanup, you still have clients with an infection, you will need to turn off those machines and contact Trend Micro Support to have them look into the problem. The usual reason for an incomplete fix is another problem with the computer that was not diagnosed beforehand, or machines without up-to-date critical updates and service packs.

- **Cleanup Now:** Will have every Agent run the Cleanup program right now. The Cleanup program is normally run with the anti-virus scan on all the Agents, so you should run this option when you have an outbreak of some type as a safety.

Settings

Outbreak Defense	Vulnerability Assessment

Automatic Outbreak Defense

☑ Enable Automatic Outbreak Defense for Red Alerts issued by Trend Micro

Disable Red Alerts after: [2 ▼] days

☑ Disable Red Alerts after required pattern/engine deployed.

Perform automatic virus scan after required component(s) deployed for:

☐ Desktops/Servers

☐ Exchange server

☐ Enable Automatic Outbreak Defense for Yellow Alerts issued by Trend Micro

Disable Yellow Alerts after: [2 ▼] days

☑ Disable Yellow Alerts after required pattern/engine deployed.

Perform automatic virus scan after required component(s) deployed for:

☐ Desktops/Servers

☐ Exchange server

We need to talk about how Trend Micro decides what an attack should be labeled as.

Yellow alerts are attacks that have been found in the wild (in the wild means in the whole world). Some of Trend Micro's customers have reported the attack. The infection does not seem to be growing and spreading at a fast rate. The attack can be dangerous and until Trend Micro gets the correct pattern files to protect you from it, they have issued basic guidelines for the WFBS sever to follow. These guidelines will only last until the next set of pattern files is downloaded to the WFBS. The Outbreak Response will end soon after the pattern files are downloaded to your server.

Red alerts are the same as a yellow alert, but the attack has been reported in numerous companies in different parts of the world. The infection is spreading and growing very fast and it is expected that it will not stop spreading anytime soon. In this case Trend Micro puts out emergency guidelines to all its customers and follows them up with pattern files and cleanup routines. The Outbreak Response will stay until the outbreak is shown to stop spreading across Trend Micro's clients. This will allow you to use both pattern file protection and the outbreak guidelines to protect your network.

We recommend that you select both Yellow and Red Alerts in your network.

Perform automatic virus scan after required component(s) deployed for:

☐ Desktops/Servers

☐ Exchange server

Always select to perform scans on both your desktops/servers and your Exchange servers. The slow down because of the scanning is well worth the confirmation that everything is ok.

☑ Disable Yellow Alerts after required pattern/engine deployed.

With Yellow alerts, we think it is safe to select the *Disable Yellow Alerts after the required pattern/engine is deployed* option.

Disable Red Alerts after: [2 ▼] days

Yellow alerts should be disabled after 2-3 days. Red alerts should be disabled after 9 days, as you want there to be at least one weekend of protection after a red alert. History has shown a second attack, usually on the weekend, following a Red alert, is common. After the weekend you can go and delete the Outbreak yourself on the first screen of Outbreak Response.

Exceptions

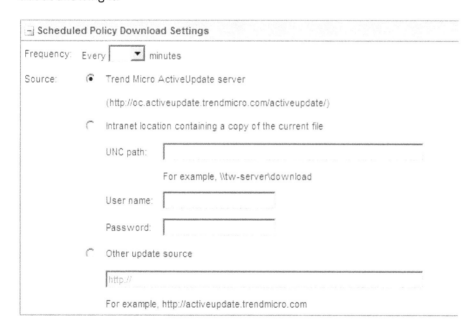

During an outbreak, you can decide if you want to leave some of the commonly blocked ports open. The only reason you should do this is because you have a business mandatory application that also uses the same port. Keeping a port open that is being attacked is a dangerous thing and you should think twice about allowing it.

Scheduling the checking for Outbreaks is done by default every 30 minutes. You can change this to between five and 120 minutes. We think 30 minutes or less is a good choice and there really is no negative from checking every five minutes if you wish.

If you utilize more than one WFBS server you can choose to have the extra WFBS check a main WFBS server by utilizing the Intranet location option. The only real use for this is if you have WFBS on your network in a place that does not have an Internet connection. If you have more than one WFBS server, it is recommend that each check the Trend Micro site for updates; this gives you a bit of redundancy.

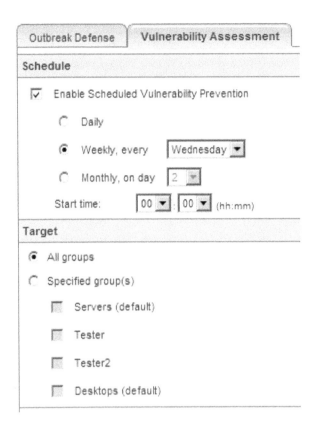

Trend Micro has included its Vulnerability Assessment tool into WFBS. The tool's job is to search the network segment in which the WFBS server is connected, to ping all computers located on the segment, and return an error if NO antivirus is found on the machine. This is a very useful tool for making sure that nobody brings a machine on your network that doesn't have virus protection.

Gotcha: By default, the system is setup to check only once a week for problem computers. We recommend checking every day and changing the time from midnight to sometime during the work day, preferably in the morning when the computers will be turned on.

You can also select what computer system types to look for but we recommend selecting them all as even a server can show up on a workstation and you want to be checking the whole network for problems.

Running a Vulnerability Assessment by hand

You can go and actually run a Vulnerability Assessment on your own to see what it does or to see if something new is on your network. To run the program, go on your Windows Explorer to

C:\Program Files\Trend Micro\Security Server\PCCSRV\Admin\Utility\TMVS

and run *TVMS.EXE.*   This tool was changed in WFBS 8 to have less features. If you want more features keep your version 7 version of the program.

To run the program, you need to insert the range of IP addresses for the segment you want to check. Click on the Start button after entering your IP address range and the program will go out and ping your network. You can watch the information on the bottom of the screen. A good way of checking the bottom without having to scroll is to click twice on the *Ping Result* `Ping result` column. This will sort all the computers the program found to the top of the list.

After finding the machines that are online, the program will then go to each address and complete an information check. Believe it or not; any program can ping any windows computer on a network and ask it pretty much anything about it. Microsoft calls this security. This is one reason why you had to buy WFBS. After a few minutes you will start to see the data for each computer fill out. You can use the bar at the bottom to go to the right and see all the data about all your computers that has been returned (this is only a small section of what was actually returned). Trend Micro will also return a result if McAfee or Symantec are located on the machines. It does not check for other anti-virus programs so if it returns that a machine has no anti-virus you will need to check to see if some other program is installed.

You can export this data for easier reading in a CSV file by clicking on the *Export* Button Export . You can now use this information to make sure all the machines currently on your network are up to your standards.

If you go into *Settings* Settings you can also automatically add the WFBS agent to all the computers you find without an anti-virus program.

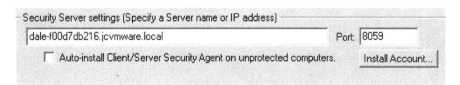

The problem here is you need to have an administrative account name and password for the machine you are trying to install the Agent on. It's a nice thought, but if someone brings a computer onto your network, odds are you won't know that info.

But there is so much more TMVS does! Let's continue.

Scheduling Scans with Windows Scheduler

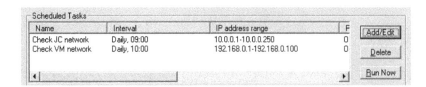

TMVS allows you to create schedules to check your segment (or other connected segments). Click on the *Add/Edit* button Add/Edit . You can then:

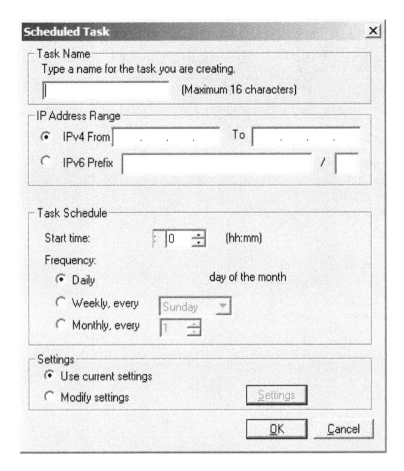

- Name your scheduled scan.
- Put in an IP range (This is great for checking numerous segments every day).
- A time of day to run (we recommend every day, during the morning).
- Utilize the current (or default) settings or make special settings for each search.

Run Now

Once you have created your searches you can wait for them to run or click on the *Run Now* button 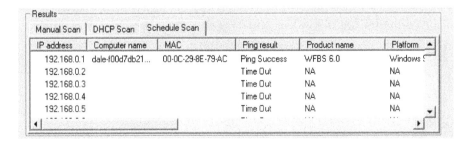.

After a search runs, the data will appear under *the Schedule Scan* Tab. Only one search set of data will stay in the window at a time.

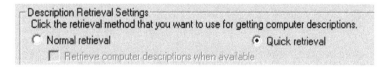

It is best to use the save as CSV options in the Settings (naming each scan a different file name) so that you can read the data offline. There are also an email option in the settings you may consider using.

Settings

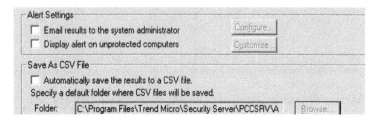

- **Check for all Trend Micro Products:** When doing a search, the search will give a positive response for all the products selected. We see no reason not to check all in this case.
- **Check for Other Antivirus Vendors:** TMVS will check for the newer versions of McAfee and Symantec. There is a hope that in the future other products will be placed in the product, but they haven't added any in the last 4-5 years.

- **Description Retrieval Settings:** This determines how deep TMVS will go when retrieving data during a scan. By default the scan is set to run a Quick retrieval. If you're doing scheduled scans and you have the time and computer utilization, we would recommend using Normal retrieval. You will get much more exact data and better checking of the data.

- **Email Results to the system administrator:** Clicking the configure button will allow you to select the From:, To:, the Subject, and the SMTP server address.

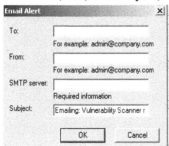

- **Display alert on unprotected computers**: An alert will be displayed on any computer that returns as not having anti-virus installed. Clicking the customize button will allow you to write out your own message for the alert. Remember that just because TMVS doesn't see a virus protection program, doesn't mean that there isn't a different one on the machine.

- **Save as a CSV File:** Allows you to create a CSV automatically whenever a scan is run (manual or scheduled). It is recommended that every scheduled scan have a different CSV name so they will not over-write each other.

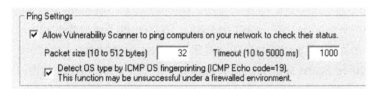

- **Ping Settings:** Only to be changed if you have a reason, but here you can change the size and timeout of the ping, along with the use of an ICMP echo request (Internet Control Message Protocol).

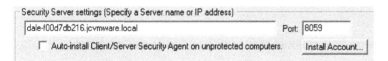

- **Security Server settings:** Here you can attempt to automatically try and install the Agent on machines that show that they do not have antivirus installed. The problem here is you will need the administrative account name and password for the machine you are trying to install the Agent on. It's a nice thought, but if someone brings a computer onto your network, odds are you won't know that info.

Chapter 5 – Scans and Updates

Manual/Scheduled Scans

Scans > Manual Scan

Select the groups to scan for security threats. If you want to modify

☑	Name
☑	Servers (default)
☑	Tester
☑	Tester2
☑	Desktops (default)
☑	2008-R2
	☑ Antivirus
	☐ Content Filtering
	☐ Attachment Blocking

[Scan Now]   [Stop Scanning]

Here you will be able to select which parts of your network on which you would like to manually run a scan. You can select which groups (or Exchange servers) you want to scan. To change the settings on each of the groups you can click on that group name. Both Manual and Scheduled scans have the same settings, with scheduling added to the Scheduled Scans section. The settings are little bit further into this chapter.

Scan Now or Stop Scanning
Under Manual scanning your only option is to select what you want to scan and click the 'Scan Now' button or the 'Stop Scanning' button.

Scheduling a Scan
Setting up a scheduled scan is exactly the same as a manual scan, except it has the addition of a Schedule tab. You will continue the setup from that spot.

Dale Johnson

Servers (default)

- ⦿ Daily
- ○ Weekly, every [Monday ▼]
- ○ Monthly, on day [1 ▼]

☑ Shut down the client after completing a Scheduled Scan

Start time: [12 ▼] : [30 ▼] (hh:mm)

You are only allowed to create one scheduled scan for each group. The schedule tab will show you a page broken down by each group. You can choose how often and at what time to start a scheduled scan. If your users leave their machines on at night you should probably do your scan at night time. If they turn them off at night, consider scanning at lunch time. All scheduled scans should always be run at low CPU Usage.

Shutdown the Client after the scan: Well you decide if you want to do this, but you can actually tell the Agents to shut down the machines they are on after a scheduled scan. Note if there is a person sitting in front of the machine they will see the option to stop the shutdown.

Settings

Agent Scans

Target	Action

- ⦿ All scannable files
- ○ IntelliScan: uses "true file type" identification ⓘ
- ○ Scan files with the following extensions (use commas to separate entries)

> .*,.ACCDB,.ARJ,.BAT,.BIN,.BOO,.CAB,.CHM,.CLA,.CLASS,.COM,.CSC,.DLL,.DOC,.DOCM,.DOCX,.D
> OT,.DOTM,.DOTX,.DRV,.EML,.EXE,.GZ,.HLP,.HTA,.HTM,.HTML,.HTT,.INI,.JAR,.JPEG,.JPG,.JS,.JSE,.L
> NK,.LZH,.MDB,.MPD,.MPP,.MPT,.MSG,.MSO,.NWS,.OCX,.OFT,.OVL,.PDF,.PHP,.PIF,.PL,.POT,.POTM,.P
> OTX,.PPAM,.PPS,.PPSM,.PPSX,.PPT,.PPTM,.PPTX,.PRC,.RAR,.REG,.RTF,.SCR,.SHS,.SYS,.TAR,.VBE,

- ☐ Scan mapped drives and shared folders on the network
- ☑ Scan compressed files: Up to [2 ▼] compression layers

Target – Select a Method – What should we scan?

We are being asked what files you should scan. Now the first thing you're going to say is, "Why don't I scan everything all the time?" Well, even though that does seem smart, there are occasions and reasons to be a bit pickier about what we scan.

- **All Scannable Files.** Simply put, if it can be scanned (it's not encrypted in some way) we will scan it, every time it moves, is opened, is saved. Everything all the time.
- **IntelliScan.** Instead of looking at the file extensions (.bat, .exe, .doc....)while scanning, we will look inside the file header to figure out what it the file really is. This is set as the Default setting and unless you have a reason should remain so.

> *Inside IntelliScan*
>
> *Not every file is as it seems. Every file has an extension. This enables Windows to determine what program should run the program. .doc files are for a word processor. .exe files are executables. But anyone can change these extensions and therefore break how Windows starts a program. How/Why? Maybe you have worked for a company that didn't let you email pictures. To get around it you could simply rename the file from .jpg to .abc. The email system is only looking for picture file extension .jpg. Since .abc isn't blocked it lets the file go. In the email you tell the person on the other end to change the extension back to .jpg to use it. IntelliScan looks inside of every file it scans for the header, which tells WFBS more about the file then just what extension it has. In the header you will see stuff like what kind of file it is, when it was created, how big it should be.... IntelliScan allows you to stop your users from breaking the system by changing extensions, and more importantly, stops hackers from hiding bad programs behind the mask of a simple and boring file extension.*

- **Scan files with the following extensions**. Here we will look at only the file extensions to determine if a file should be virus checked. If you select this option you can edit the data inside the box to add or subtract extensions. We do not recommend this option unless you really, really have a good reason. After you think you have a good reason, you should then call someone to talk you out of it.
- **Scan Compressed Files up to X layers.** Ah, we talked about this just a minute ago. Now you have to consider how much computer time and utilization it takes to unzip a zip file 20 times to find that .exe file. It takes a lot. So, here we are going to limit the layers of compression to check for normal compressed files that IntelliTrap has already Ok'd or ignored because it doesn't see a problem. Want to move it up to 6 (the limit)? Go for it. Odds are you will never even see a zip file that layered, but if you do you might as well check it.

Dale Johnson

Exclusions:

Enable Exclusions

Do not scan the following directories:

Do not scan the directories where Trend Micro products are installed.

Enter the directory path (E.g. c:\temp\ExcludeDir)

Add

Delete

Do not scan the following files:

Enter the file name or the file name with full path
(E.g. ExcludeDoc.hlp; c:\temp\excldir\ExcludeDoc.hlp)

Add

Delete

Directories: Not everything on the computer needs to be checked. Some things are a waste of time. A good example on a server is an Exchange or SQL Database. They are encrypted and scanning them will do nothing. WFBS allows us to either exclude files or whole directories. You should be careful about directories and ONLY exclude them on servers. One would hope that your server has good permissions set up so only specific processes can write to specific directories (Exchange is the only process that can write to the Exchange database directory).

File Names: There are also files you won't want scanned. Windows has a few that you might consider, but overall scanning them won't hurt anything and WFBS has a list of windows files it already knows to ignore. So what you should be interested here is if WFBS does anything funky with a homemade program you run on some or all of your workstations. The best example I have seen over the years is either your human resources or your accounting programs. These programs are notorious for doing funky things with databases and how they run on your computer. If you have these problems determined by yourself or with Trends Micro's help, you can put them in here.

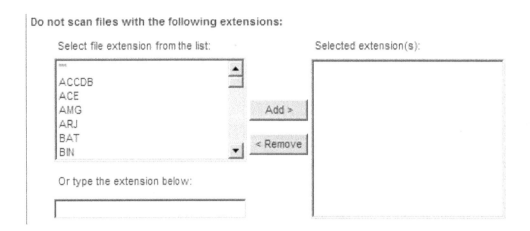

File Extensions: Excluding file extensions is a bit more dangerous. Here you would be overriding the IntelliScan option you set above by saying never scan any file with the following extension, even if it is another program hiding as this extension. Again, if you find a program or file type that is being a problem, put it in here, but don't do that unless you are sure that it is the problem.

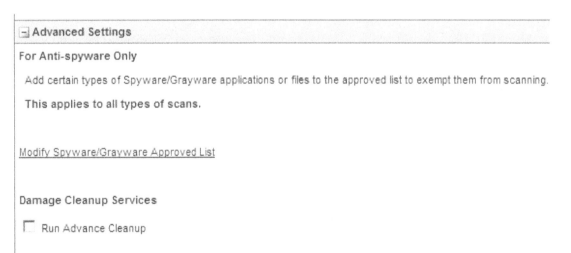

Modify Spyware/Grayware Approved List: Here you can add any programs you think need to be ignored by WFBS during a spyware scan.

Run Advanced Cleanup: You hate FakeAV. We hate FakeAV. Everyone hates FakeAV except the FakeAV folks. This option will basically stop the processes like those of FakeAV and get rid of it. TURN THIS ON NOW!

CPU Usage

The period of time Security Server waits between scanning each file affects CPU usage. Select a lower CPU usage level to CPU to perform other tasks.

○ High: scan files one after another without pausing

◉ Medium: pausing between file scans if CPU consumption is higher than 50%, and do not pause if 50% or lower

○ Low: pausing between file scans if CPU consumption is higher than 20%, and do not pause if 20% or lower

- **CPU Usage**: The choice of how much CPU usage you use depends on why you are doing a manual scan. If you are doing a scan just for some routine reason then you should select the Low option and not bother your users. If you are working on an emergency it would be best to take the High option and make sure there are no existing problems on your machines.

- **ActiveAction:** In the Actions tab, you will tell WFBS what to do when you encounter a problem. The default setting (Letting WFBS decide) is ActiveAction. In the last 10 years, viruses have become un-cleanable. Back in the 1990's viruses would try to infect a single file. Those files were sometimes cleanable, and you could actually use the file after cleaning the virus out of it. As virus writers have progressed, they no longer look into infecting single files, but have progressed into infecting your process DLLs and EXEs. So, Trend Micro has developed a system that determines by each infection type how to deal with the files infected. Some clients have found these settings to screw up their files and use the manual configuration noted below to setup their Agents. We recommend using Active Action if you're not sure about what options to choose and want to take the safe and simple option.

○ Customized action for the following detected threats

Restore Defaults

Type	Action
Joke	Quarantine ▼
Worm/Trojans	Quarantine ▼
Packer	Quarantine ▼
Probable malware	Quarantine ▼
Virus	Clean ▼
Spyware/Grayware	Clean ▼
Test Virus	Pass ▼
Other malware	Clean ▼

- **Customized Action:** If you want to choose to configure your own you will have a choice of what you want to do with the different types of infections. We recommend you delete any Trojan, Spyware, or Packer.   You should also either quarantine or delete the rest of the options (Generic, Virus, or Other).   As was mentioned in the above paragraph, very little can be done to infected files, so either quarantining or outright deleting them seems the best.

☐ **Advanced Settings**

☐ Display an alert message on the desktop or server when a virus/spyware is detected

☐ Display an alert message on the desktop or server when a probable virus/spyware is detected

☐ Run cleanup when probable virus/malware is detected

- **Advanced Settings:**
  ○ **Display alert messages on desktop:** Do you want the users to know every time they have triggered a virus or spyware? This has its good points, keeping the users knowing when they are doing or when they are going to bad places. But it can be a Help Desk nightmare for some users.   You might consider breaking your users up into two groups and having different options for each: Users I can deal with, and users I can't.
  ○ **Display alert message for probable virus/spyware:** If by chance WFBS thinks it has found something wrong before it goes off and possibly cleans the problem it will alert the user that it has found something wrong and is going to try and fix it. You should probably only turn this on for users who actually understand what is happening.
  ○ **Run cleanup when probable virus/spyware:** If the system finds that probable virus here it will go and try and fix it. It will ONLY do this if you choose ActiveAction and selected an action previously on this screen.

Antivirus

Default Scan

Select a method for scanning viruses, worms, Trojans, and other malicious code:

- ⦿ All attachment files
- ○ IntelliScan: uses "true file type" identification ⓘ
- ○ ⊞ Specific file types
- ☑ Enable IntelliTrap ⓘ
- ☑ Scan message body

You need to choose which files to scan. All scannable files is the default.

- **All Attachment Files.** Simply put, if it has an attachment it will be scanned (it's not encrypted in some way) we will scan it, every time it moves, is opened, is saved. Everything all the time.
- **IntelliScan.** Instead of looking at the file extensions (.bat, .exe, .doc....)while scanning, we will look inside the file header to figure out what it the file really is. This is set as the Default setting and unless you have a reason should remain so.

  Inside IntelliScan

  Not every file is as it seems. Every file has an extension. This enables Windows to determine what program should run the program. .doc files are for a word processor. .exe files are executables. But anyone can change these extensions and therefore break how Windows starts a program. How/Why? Maybe you have worked for a company that didn't let you email pictures. To get around it you could simply rename the file from .jpg to .abc. The email system is only looking for picture file extension .jpg. Since .abc isn't blocked it lets the file go. In the email you tell the person on the other end to change the extension back to .jpg to use it. IntelliScan looks inside of every file it scans for the header, which tells WFBS more about the file then just what extension it has. In the header you will see stuff like what kind of file it is, when it was created, how big it should be.... IntelliScan allows you to stop your users from breaking the system by changing extensions, and more importantly, stops hackers from hiding bad programs behind the mask of a simple and boring file extension.

- **Specific file types**. Here we will look at only the file extensions to determine if a file should be virus checked. If you select this option you can edit the data inside the box to add or subtract extensions. We do not recommend this option unless you really, really have a good reason. After you think you have a good reason, you should then call someone to talk you out of it.

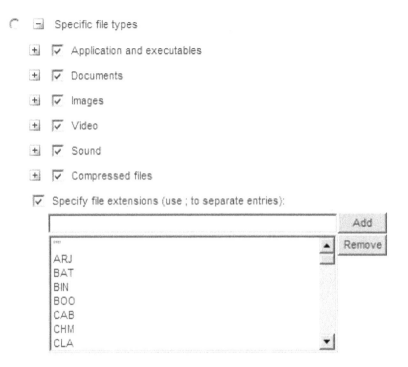

- **IntelliTrap**. One way of hiding a virus is to compress it numerous times into a file. This can be an effective hack because your antivirus software is set to ignore compressed files with over *X* number of compressions. This is set on by default.

  In less nerdy terms, if I take an exe program and compress it into a zip file, it really doesn't do anything but it does change the file extension to .zip and now the header is a .zip file. So the exe is hidden behind the zip file and can only be found if the zip is opened. WFBS will check inside the zip file and look at the exe file to virus-check it. But what if someone keeps zipping the zip file, say 14 times? If so, your computer looks at the zip file and sees:

  .zip -> .zip -> .zip -> .zip -> .zip -> .zip -> .zip -> .zip -> .zip -> .zip -> .zip -> .zip -> .zip -> .zip -> .exe

  Some virus protection programs (this one included) will allow you to choose how many levels of that zip file (or any compressed file) to look into before giving up. If the .exe is hidden deep enough, the virus protection will give up!

  IntelliTrap allows the WFBS to look into the compressed file, look real deep (20 layers or so), and check to see if anything is hiding. Different compression programs have different rules about levels of compression. IntelliTrap has a database of compressions types and is better than you at trying to figure it out.

- **Scan Message Body:** Email messages can contain MIME based embedded data. For this reason, it is possible that a virus could be in the body of a message. You should always leave this option turned on.

Additional Threat Scans

```
Additional Threat Scan

☐  Select All

   ☑  Spyware                          ☑  Adware

   ☐  Dialers                          ☐  Joke Programs

   ☐  Hacking Tools                    ☐  Remote Access Tools

   ☐  Password Cracking Applications   ☐  Others
```

We are offering to stop other bad types of emails. By default, the system has only selected Spyware and Adware. We think it would be smart to select all of these expect for Others, which really is a bit of a tossup. Exactly what are these options?

- **Spyware:** Programs that install on your computer capture data (usually key strokes) and send the data to a server somewhere in the world to be abused. Some of these are also known as Keyloggers.
- **Dialers:** Not used much these days, but before broad-band we all used to connect to the internet with a modem. To do this, the modem needed a dialer. Some enterprising people figured out if they could make you use their dialer, they could charge you some ridiculous cost per minute to connect to the internet.
- **Hacking Tools:** The name pretty much says it. If a hacker can get a hacker tool on your computer, they can hack it.
- **Password Cracking Applications:** Replaced mostly by more powerful keyloggers, these programs would attempt to figure out your system passwords.
- **Adware:** Programs that put advertisements pretty much everywhere on your computer. These started soon after the beginning of the Internet and will never go away.
- **Joke Programs:** These programs usually don't do real harm (but they have been known to occasionally), but they tend to scare the user into thinking something is wrong with their computer, their car, or the world.
- **Remote Access Tools:** Programs that once installed by a hacker will allow them to take your computer over remotely. Very dangerous.
- **Others:** Other programs and bad things defined by Trend Micro.

Exclusions

Do not scan attachment and/or message body if:

☑	Message body size exceeds:	30	MB
☑	Attachment size exceeds:	30	MB

Do not scan compressed files if:

☑	Decompressed file count exceeds:	9999	(1-10000)
☑	Size of decompressed file exceeds:	100	MB
☑	Number of layers of compression exceeds:	5	(1-20)
☑	Size of decompressed file is "x" times the size of compressed file:	1000	(100-1000000)

You can also stop messages from entering the Exchange server by defining limits to the message. Administrators used to limit message and attachments sizes more often when hard drives were expensive to buy and maintain. In these days of Terabyte drives for under $100, these options are used less. But if your server has free space problems you may consider using them. These are turned on by default, you can turn them off by un-clicking them.

- **Message body size exceeds:** Will stop any message with a message body over X amount of size from being accepted into the server. It is not normal for a message body to be of that size or contain that many embedded parts. Default is 30MB
- **Attachment size exceeds:** Will stop any message with a combined attachment size over X amount of size from being accepted into the server. If you routinely send large files, then you will need to turn off this option. Default is 30MB
- **Compressed file scanning:** The secret of understanding why this is an option has to do with the word large. Hackers tend to go for small, quiet, quick attacks on your computer. Over email they can make the attack a little bigger without you noticing. Scanning large compressed files is a large drain on the MSA. Because of the time and utilization wasted, MSA has the option to stop scanning files over a certain size, and to only scan so many layers of the compressed file.
- **Decompressed file count exceeds:** Do not scan a compressed file (let it proceed) if there are more than X number of files contained in the file. Default is 9999, which is probably a bit high. Maybe 5000 is a good number.
- **Size of decompressed file exceeds:** If, after uncompressing (decompressing happens after diving in the ocean) the files, one of the files will exceed X MB in size. This is a weird setting (not just the name of it). One large file in a compressed file will let the rest of the compressed file through. Seems like an easy way for hackers to go around the system. Default is 100MB, we recommend turning this option off.
- **Number of layers of compression exceeds:** Now we have to consider how much computer time and utilization it takes to unzip a zip file 20 times to find that exe file. It takes a lot. So here we

are going to limit the layers of compression to check for normal compressed files that IntelliTrap has already Ok'd or ignored because it doesn't see a problem. Want to move it up to 6? Go for it. 20? That will cause the message to really slow down the system. Default is 5, we think 5-6 is a good number to use.

- **Size of decompressed files is "X" times the size of compressed files:** If a file expands X number of times when it is uncompressed, then it didn't really contain much information in the first place. Again this is a good way for a hacker to get around the system and we recommend it be turned off. Default is 1000.

Antivirus Actions

| Target | **Action** |

⦿ ActiveAction

ActiveAction performs the Trend Micro recommended action. 🛈

○ Customized action for the following detected threats:

  ○ Perform the same action for all detected Internet threats

  All detected threats: [Clean ▾]

  ⦿ Specify action per detected threat

  Viruses: [Clean ▾]

  Worms/Trojans: [Replace with text/file ▾]

  Packers: [Quarantine message part ▾]

  Other malicious code: [Clean ▾]

  Additional threats: [Replace with text/file ▾]

  ☑ Enable action on Mass-mailing behavior (This overwrites all other actions.)

  Mass-mailing: [Replace with text/file ▾]

  Messages will be quarantined to the Quarantine directory.

Do this when clean is unsuccessful: [Replace with text/file ▾]

☐ Backup infected file before performing action

☑ Do not clean infected compressed files to optimize performance. 🛈

- **ActiveAction:** In the Actions tab you will tell WFBS what to do when you encounter a problem. The default setting (letting WFBS decide) is by far the best choice. In the last several years viruses have become un-cleanable. Back in the 1990's, viruses would try to infect a single file. Those files were sometimes cleanable, and you could actually use the file after cleaning the virus out of it. As Virus writers have progressed, they no longer look into infecting single files, but have progressed into infecting your process DLLs and EXEs. So Trend Micro has developed a system that determines by each infection type how to deal with the files infected. These change daily and we highly recommend taking Trend Micro's ActiveAction decisions.

- **Customized Attacks:** Here we can choose how we want to handle infections when we find them. Let's look at the different threats.
    - **Viruses:** Any file found trying to infect your system or a file.
    - **Worms/Trojans:** These are attacks on your system. Instead of just infecting our system, these lovelies will install programs on your system and run processes in the background. Sometimes you will know something is wrong, sometimes it will hide and gather data.
    - **Packers:** A Packer is a method of getting Worms, Trojans or Root Kits onto your system. The idea is to hide the .EXE that starts the infection inside of compression files.
    - **Other malicious code:** Assorted programs that will do something bad to your system.
    - **Additional threats:** Additional problems listed in Trend Micro's database.
    - **Mass-mailing behavior:** Not as used as it once was, the idea is to infect your Microsoft Outlook program so that it will send out mass mailing of spam to your contact list. Getting the spam message to be sent from you to someone you know, allows the spammer to get a better chance of it being read. Mass mailings can contain more than words, including things like Trojans and worms.
- **Customized Actions:** Now let's look at the different things you can do to the message that is found infected. Note that email messages are handled differently than desktop viruses because Microsoft Exchange has certain demands on the antivirus program.
    - **Clean:** Clean the infection and follow the "Do this when clean is unsuccessful" Do this when clean is unsuccessful: [Delete entire message ▼] selection lower on the screen.
    - **Replace with text/file:** If an attachment is found infected, delete it and replace it with a text file. The message will then be sent along with the fake attachment. The information in the text file is customized further down the page.
    - **Quarantine entire message:** This will automatically send the message along with attachments into quarantine. The user will not receive any notification of quarantine.
    - **Delete entire message:** Deletes the entire message, with no notification.
    - **Pass:** Let the message go (not something we recommend).
    - **Quarantine the message part:** Sends the infected attachment to quarantine, but sends the rest of the message along with no note of the deletion.

We recommend choosing *Replace with text/file* or *Quarantine the message*.

- **Do this when clean is unsuccessful:** Choose what to do when you selected either:
    - Clean as an option above
    - ActiveAction
- **Backup infected file before performing action**: This is a safety that will back up the file before taking the infected attachment apart for cleaning. If you have problems with clean files being corrupted you should turn this option on. If you're deleting or replacing infected attachments it

won't do anything turned on. You can elect what directory to back the files up to further down the page. It is not selected by default.

- **Do not clean infected compressed files to optimize performance**: This option looks at the attachment; if it is a compressed file of some type it will simply delete the attachment and send the message along. This option is selected by default and although it makes sense not to spend all that time trying to scan a compressed file; however, if your users do send compressed files back and forth it may be a bad option to turn on.

Notification

Notification
☐ Notify recipients ⊟
☐ Do not notify external recipients
☐ Notify senders ⊟
☐ Do not notify external senders
☑ Disable sender notifications for spoofing emails

Whom do you want to notify that a virus was found and dealt with?

- Notify recipients: Sends a note to all recipients listed on the message (To, CC, and BCC) is sent. Most people turn this option on; it is off by default.
- Do not notify external recipients: If recipients do not have a mailbox on the server, do not send them a message. The scenario you would use this is if your internal users are sending out viruses, you probably do not want to let your customers know you're infected. This is not selected by default.
- Notify Senders: Notify the senders of a message that they are infected. Some administrators like to do this and some don't bother. We recommend you turn this on if your customer base sends lots of attachments to your users. It is not selected by default.
- Do not notify external senders: As just explained, we recommend this on if you have large attachments coming from your customers. This is not selected by default.
- Disable sender notifications for spoofing emails: A spoofing email is when person named in the from line of the message is not the actual person who sent it. It is easy for an email program (or spammer) to change the from address to anything they want. MSA can verify if a message is spoofing one of its own users. How? Well if the message says it was created by you and it wasn't created by the Exchange server, then it must be spoofed.

Macros

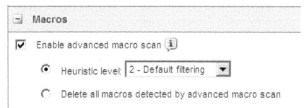

Attaching viruses into documents via the use of macros is a very effective way of getting abusive programs onto a workstation.   You should enable this option, as it is by default.

- **Heuristic Level:** Looks dead into the macro, defines what the macro is going to do and chooses if this falls within certain levels which we can select. The leveling is set from lenient filtering to rigorous filtering.   The higher the filtering level, the more time will be taken to tear apart the macro and the stricter the filter will be in deciding if the macro is bad. The default is set to 2 (Default filtering) and is recommend to stay at this level unless you have had problems either not catching or catching too many macro viruses.

- **Delete all macros by advanced macro scan:** If a macro is found the macro is deleted. This is pretty hard stuff as most people use macros effectively day to day. This is not selected by default and unless you have a severe problem, should not be.

Unscannable Message Parts

What happens when you get an attachment that is either encrypted or password protected?   Since there is no way for this file to be virus checked, most administrators would just pass it along. If you use encrypted mail, then you must pass the files.   We recommend pass as the choice, unless you're being infected by password protected files.

Excluded Message Parts

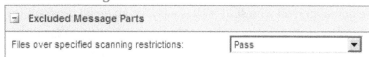

What do you do with attachments that were found too big or have too many compressed files earlier on this page? Most administrators would pass the attachments as they simply don't expect very large attachments to be infected. You could quarantine the attachments if you think that there could be a problem and if you will want to get to the attachment if it is actually good. By default the setting is set to Pass.

Backup Setting

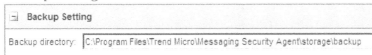

If you have chosen earlier to backup files before you clean them, you can select here where you would like to place those encrypted files. By default the directory is set to

C:\Program Files\Trend Micro\Messaging Security Agent\storage\backup

Replacement Settings

If you have selected at any time to replace an attachment with a Text/File or chosen ActiveAction, we can customize the message that we put in that replace text file. When the user gets the message and sees the attachment (named VIRUS_DETECTED_AND_REMOVED.TXT), they can open it and see the text typed in here.

In content filtering, you look at the insides of the message; where is it from, what does it say, what is attached and determine if you are going to stop the message.

- **Enable content filtering**: Turn this module on or off.
- **Adding a new Filter** ☐ Add . Not for the average person, but if you want to add a filter you can create a list of definitions to check the message with. You can use this filter to either add to the blocking rules or use it to define messages you know are good. If you are going to do this, we recommend you employ the WFBS manual on how to do this. We will only gloss over these options in this book.

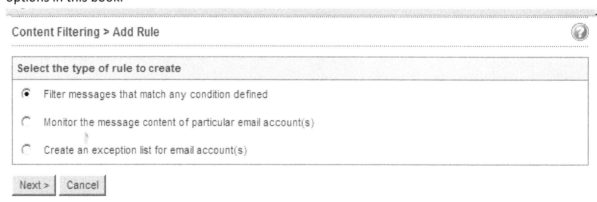

- **Filter Type**: We can choose what type of filter we want to use.

Filter messages that match any condition defined:

You will have a list of conditions; if any are found then you need to trigger this message to do what you want. This is good for finding information that can be in any message.

Choose which parts of the message to search

Chose the words to add, if they should be case sensitive, and list any synonyms you may want to also add.

What are you going to do with these messages, including:

- Replacing the message with a default message you can create yourself.
- Quarantining or deleting the message.
- Archiving the message into a directory and delivering the message as normal (This is called spying).
- Along with action you performed to the message, notifying either the sender or recipient a message saying you performed it.

Archiv
e Settings: You can change where the messages and their attachments will be archived during this process. This allows you to have different locations for different filters and allow different people to see the different archives. Note HR might want this option.

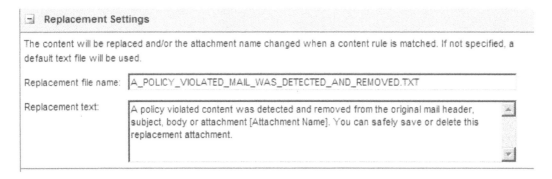

Replacement Settings: You can also create a file that has will replace the blocked attachment and call it and put in it what you want. In Exchange any attachment that is blocked must be replaced with another file.

Monitor the message content of particular email account(s):

Here we are going to look for an email address in either the From:, To: or CC: of the message.

What email addresses do you want to search for and in what part of the message? Adding Joe to all the parts means we are watching for all of Joe's emails.

Are you going to search the message for any particular words?

What are we going to do with these messages, including:

- Replacing the message with a default message you can create yourself.
- Quarantining or deleting the message
- Archiving the message into a directory and delivering the message as normal (This is called spying)
- Along with action you performed to the message, notifying either the sender or recipient a message saying you performed it.
-

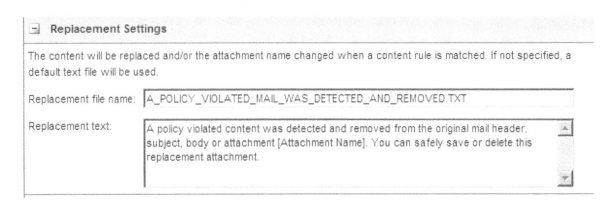

Archive Settings: You can change where the messages and their attachments will be archived during this process. This allows you to have different locations for different blocks and allow different people to see the different archives. Note HR might enjoy this.

Replacement Settings: You can also create a file that has will replace the blocked attachment and call it and put in it what you want. In Exchange any attachment that is blocked must be replaced with another file.

Create an exception list for email account(s):

Here you will create a list of people who you don't want to control their mail. Usually you would include the top bosses or someone like that in the company.

List the users you want in this rule.

Content Filtering > Add Rule

Rule name: | Execption

Messaging Security Agent does not apply content rules with a lower priority than this ru accounts in this list

Specify an email account list exception rule:

	Add
Curly@jconsult.com	Remove
Larry@jconsult.com	
Moe@jconsult.com	
	Import

< Back | Finish | Cancel

When you are done you should reorder this rule to Number 1 so it runs before all the other rules.

Attachment Blocking:
Allows us to block attachments by type, name or existence of a zip file.

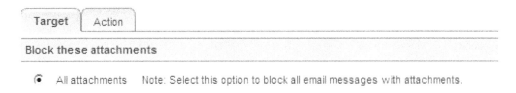

| Target | Action |

Block these attachments

⊙ All attachments   Note: Select this option to block all email messages with attachments.

All Attachment: Will block every message that has any attachment

- ⊟ ☐ Attachment types to exclude
    - ⊞ ☐ Application and executables
    - ⊞ ☐ Documents
    - ⊞ ☐ Images
    - ⊞ ☐ Video
    - ⊞ ☐ Sound
    - ⊞ ☐ Compressed files

Attachment Types: Will allow you to select exactly what type of attachment you want to block

- ⊟ ☐ Attachment names to exclude
    - ☐ Specific file extensions to exclude (use ; to separate entries)

    [_____] [Add]
    [   ] [Remove]
    [   ]
    [   ]
    [   ]

    - ☐ Attachment names to exclude

    [_____] [Add]
    [   ] [Remove]
    [   ]
    [   ]
    [   ]

Attachment Names to Exclude: What attachment extensions or actual names do you want to exclude from your above types rules.

○ Specific attachments

⊟ ☐ Attachment types

    ⊟ ☐ Application and executables

        ☐ Executable and Linking Format (.elf)

        ☐ Executable (.exe; .dll; .vxd)

        ☐ JAVA Applet (.class)

        ☐ Windows NT/95 shortcut (.lnk)

        ☐ Windows Installer Package (.msi)

    ⊞ ☐ Documents

    ⊞ ☐ Images

    ⊞ ☐ Video

    ⊞ ☐ Sound

    ⊞ ☐ Compressed files

Specific Attachments: Choose exactly what attachments should be stopped

⊟ ☐ Attachment names

    ☐ Specific file extensions to block (use ; to separate entries)

	Add
ADE	Remove
ADP	
ASX	
BAS	
BAT	
BIN	
CHM	

    ☐ Attachment names to block

	Add
	Remove

Attachment Names: Exactly what attachment names do you want to exclude.

☐ Block attachment types or names within ZIP files

Block attachment types and names within zip files: If a message has a zip file, take it apart to make sure that no files are in their breaking our rules. This will not check passworded zip files or encrypted files at all.

What are you going to do with these messages, including:

- Replacing the message with a default message you can create yourself.
- Quarantining or deleting the message
- Along with action you performed to the message, notifying either the sender or recipient a message saying you performed it.

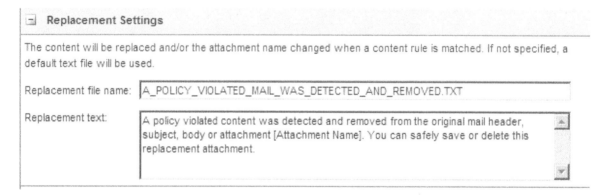

Replacement Settings: You can also create a file that has will replace the blocked attachment and call it and put in it what you want. In Exchange any attachment that is blocked must be replaced with another file.

Updates

How do Trend Micro updates work?

- The WFBS program contacts a Trend Micro server and downloads a server.ini file. You can see this file for yourself. It lives in *C:\Program Files\Trend Micro\Security Server\PCCSRV\Download*.
- WFBS then scans the file for data on each part of WFBS that can be updated, and compares it to the current installed list.
- A list of needed updates is made, and WFBS does a download of each file that is new and requested.
- Once the file is downloaded it is de-compressed and placed on the server in the directory *C:\Program Files\Trend Micro\Security Server\PCCSRV*.
- Now WFBS determines which files need to go out to the different Workstations and Servers. It upgrades its database with the information.
- The next time the Workstation or Server connects to WFBS (every 120 minutes by default) they will ask the server if it has new updates.
- When it receives notification that updates await, it will download the updates and install them locally.

Manual Update

What files would you like to update? Choose your files and select '*Update*'.

Update Results

Security Server is updating the following components right now. This may take a few minutes.

Status

Component	Progress		Status
Messaging Security Agent			
Messaging Security Agent Anti-spam pattern		100%	No Updates Available
Messaging Security Agent Anti-spam engine 32-bit		100%	No Updates Available
Messaging Security Agent Anti-spam engine 64-bit		100%	No Updates Available
Messaging Security Agent scan engine 32-bit		100%	No Updates Available
Messaging Security Agent scan engine 64-bit		100%	No Updates Available
Messaging Security Agent URL filtering engine 32-bit		100%	No Updates Available
Messaging Security Agent URL filtering engine 64-bit		100%	No Updates Available
Antivirus			
Virus Pattern		100%	Successful

Scheduled Updates

Scheduling updates behaves the same as manual updates expect for the addition of a Schedule Tab.

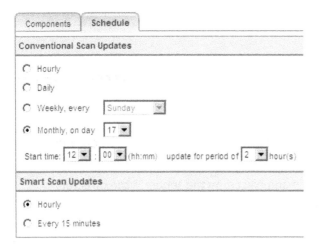

It is recommended you select hourly. You will want the system to check for updates often so that your pattern files are up to date.

Smart Scan Updates: Will update your smart scan server with the latest pattern and Cleanup patterns. We recommend choosing every 15 minutes.

Update Source

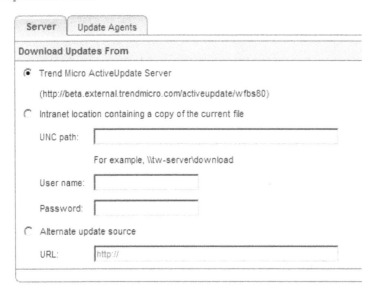

By default (and you should keep it set this way) WFBS will go to a Trend Micro server on the Internet to check for updates. You can utilize Intranet locations or alternative update sources if you have multiple WFBS servers.

One of the more unique options in WFBS is to create downstream Update Agents.   Let's take a look at what that means.

In our example, we will use an organization with three offices.   The main office (in Woburn, MA) maintains the large connection to the Internet and all of the servers. Each of the branch offices (Charlotte and Atlanta) has four or five users and only a small file server. So for anything to be updated from these small offices, they need to contact the main office over the small wan connection they have installed between the offices. The problem is that connection is used pretty much just to maintain your business applications. If your workstations had to check and possibly download a new update every few hours it wouldn't be very good for your network.

WFBS's solution is to create a machine in both Charlotte and Atlanta and call it an Update Agent. This Update Agent will connect to the Main WFBS server to get the updates, and then the downstream machines in the same office will connect to it to get their updates. So instead of four or five connections up to the main office, we now have one. This does add another step to the update process and means an update may take four hours to get to the end workstation instead of two. But in an emergency, when you hit the update now button, the update alert from the WFBS will be sent directly to the Update Agents and they will immediately send an update to their local workstations.

When you set up this scenario, you must create groups for each office and place each of the machines in that location in that group.

Now we can go to the Updates -> Source -> Security Agents Tab and into the Assign Update Agents section. Click on the *Add* button to create an Update Agent

Select security agent(s) from the list to assign them as update agent(s).

Select the machine in the group you want to build the Update Agent in (Charlotte or Atlanta). The Agent will now appear in the Assign Update Agents. A message will be sent down to the machines and the Update Agent part of the WFBS Agent will be turned on. The next time the other machines in the same group contact the main WFBS server, they will be given direction to connect to the Update Agent in their group.

If by chance the Update Agent machine goes down or out of service, the machines in the group will revert to contacting the WFBS server while they can't connect the local Update Agent. You can then setup a new Update Agent and remove the out-of-service machine from *Assign Updates Agents* screen.

Security Agent Alternative Update Source

This is a bit confusing, but let's gets through it. Let's change the scenario a bit and add another office in Concord, NC. It will connect directly to the Charlotte office and only have two employees. Now we don't really want to make one of those machines an Update Agent. We don't want them going all the way through both lines back to Woburn. So we have two choices: We can add them to the Charlotte group, or we can tell them to use an Alternative Update Source.

Enable the option and click on the Add button  .

We would enter in the IP range of the machines we want to re-direct. Then we can enter either the name of an Update Agent or a specified ActiveUpdate server.

Here is the cool part. If you place http://wfbs60-p.activeupdate.trendmicro.com/activeupdate as the update source, the machines will go to Trend Micro to get their updates. This is an excellent alternative for an office all by itself with no connection to the main office. But there is one gotcha with this setup. Those machines will never contact the WFBS server, and will never get configuration updates or Outbreak Defense alerts. If you can live with those limits you may have just found a good way of setting up a separate office with WFBS Agents.

Chapter 6 – Reporting and Logs

You can use reporting to manually create reports, or to schedule the making of reports. Your reports can then be saved and you can send them to your inbox. One version (copy) of the manual reports and numerous versions of the scheduled reports are saved on the server. You can look up previous reports via the console and in the directory:

C:\Program Files\Trend Micro\Security Server\PCCSRV\Download\Report

One-time (Manual) Reports

'One-time reports' is a misnaming. You can actually save these reports and use them multiple times. So we will use the phrase 'Manual Reports'. Let's start by making a new report by clicking on the *Add* button.

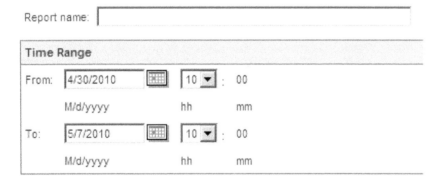

Type in your Report name and select a time range for the data you want to look at.

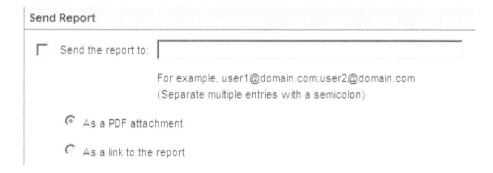

Content	□ Select all	
± □	Antivirus	
□	Outbreak Defense History	
± □	Anti-spyware	
□	Anti-spam summary	
□	Web Reputation	
□	URL category	
□	Behavior Monitoring	
□	Device Control	
± □	Content Filtering	
± □	Network Virus	

You can now select which type of reports you would like to receive. In a bit, we will go through what all these options mean.

Send Report

□ Send the report to: [   ]

For example, user1@domain.com;user2@domain.com
(Separate multiple entries with a semicolon)

⊙ As a PDF attachment

○ As a link to the report

By default, your report will be created in a PDF and you will be able to see it on the first screen we started at. If you want to send the report to yourself or someone else (and you have the SMTP setup), you can either attach the report as a PDF or send a link to the user so they can see or download the report from the WFBS server.

Scheduled Reports

Reports > Scheduled Reports

	Report Template	Next Report On	Frequency	History	Enabled
□	Spam Spam Spam Spam - Weekly	5/9/2010 0:10:00	Weekly	Report History	⊙
□	Weekly Viruses	5/9/2010 0:10:00	Weekly	Report History	⊙

Adding a scheduled report is the same as adding a manual report. The only addition is the need to define a schedule for the report.

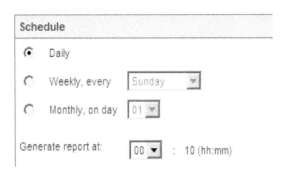

If you do not include sending the report via email, it will simply appear on the scheduled report screen for you to review later. In the Report Maintenance section you can determine how many of these reports to save.

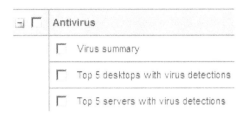

- **Virus Summary**: Will give you the basic counts on what types of viruses have been found and cleaned. MSA virus data will be created on its own page.
- **Top 5 Desktops/Servers with Virus Detections**: Both of these options produce a list of each type and a count of viruses found.

Outbreak Defense History

- **Outbreak Defense History**: If you have used and received an Outbreak Defense, this report will give you a rundown of the last defense history.

- **Spyware/Grayware Summary**: A list of which types of Spyware and Grayware were found.

Anti-spam summary

- **Anti-spam summary**: From the MSA, this will produce a count of Spam, Phishes and total message count.

Web Reputation

- **Web Reputation**: A list of which ten machines have most often abused the Web Reputation rules

- **URL Category**: A listing of the five most abused URL policies and the top ten machines abusing all the URL policies. It does not give a cross between the two sets, telling you which machines abused which policies.

- **Behavior Monitoring**: A listing of the five most abused behavior policies and the top ten machines abusing all the behavior policies. It does not give a cross between the two sets, telling you which machines abused which behaviors.

☐ Device Control

- **Device Control**: Produces a report showing the top five programs and the top ten computers that violated the policies.

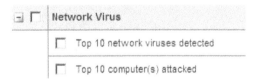

- **Content Filtering Summary**: Gives you a total message count of the MSA along with how many messages were stopped because of violating content filtering policies.
- **Top 10 Content Filtering Rules Violated**: A list of the top ten content filtering rules blocked by the MSA.

☐ Network Virus
   ☐ Top 10 network viruses detected
   ☐ Top 10 computer(s) attacked

- **Top 10 Network Viruses Detected**: A list of the top 10 network viruses blocked by the Agents.
- **Top 10 Computers Attacked**: List of the top 10 machines that had an attack blocked.

Instead of dealing with a long report, we can do a simple search of our log files.

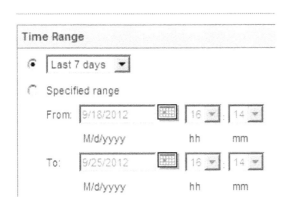

Select when you want to do your search. The speed of the search is directly related to how long you select to search. Also, you are limited in the search by how long you keep log files. By default you keep 30 days of log files.

Type: You can choose which kind of log file you would like to search.

1. **Management console events:** This log file contains information on what happens to the WFBS console, scans, Outbreak Defense events, and updates to the server.

2. **Desktop/Server:**   What has happened on your Agents, broken down into the different types of protection.

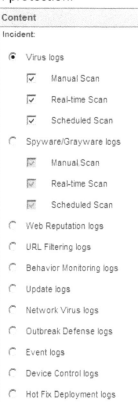

3. **Exchange Server:** A log of the different events that have occurred on your MSA

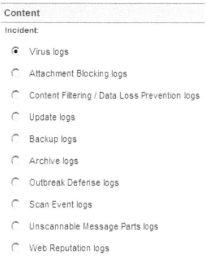

A search will create an HTML report which can also be saved as a CSV file. The file will be lost after you leave the report webpage.   Once you start a search you will not be able to stop the event, so please be careful about searching for huge amounts of data during a span of time.

Report/Log Maintenance

Report Maintenance

Reports > Maintenance

Report Type	Maximum Reports to Keep (1-100)
One-time reports	10
Scheduled reports saved in each template	10
Report templates	10

Here you can determine how many old reports you want to automatically keep on the server.   Note that each report can take upwards of 300KB of space. Reports are in this directory:
C:\Program Files\Trend Micro\Security Server\PCCSRV\Download\Report

Auto Log Deletion

The WFBS maintains a good deal of log files and they can take up a good deal of space.   Here, you can decide how long you want to keep each of these files for searching and reports.   This page will tell you the beginning and end date of any data entered in the log files.   Reports are broken into groups

- **Security Server:** Log files containing information on what has happened on the console, manual scan logs data, and when items have been updated
- **Desktops/Servers:** Log files retrieved from your Agents.
- **Exchange Server(s):** Log files retrieved from your MSA.

How long will you allow log files to stay on your server is mostly related with your free hard drive space. The more users you have, the longer you keep the logs, the more space log files will take. Although the logs are pretty useless to look at directly, they are located here:

C:\Program Files\Trend Micro\Security Server\PCCSRV\Log

Manual Log Deletion

Using the same logs files as we did in the Auto Log Deletion, the Manual Delete allows you to select a log file, choose a number of days you want to keep, and delete all log data older than that number of days.

Chapter 7 Preferences

In the preferences chapter, you will learn at how you can configure the server, and how to make sure the license is up to date.

Event Notifications

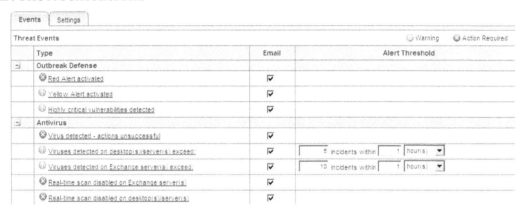

Here, you will determine when you want to be alerted (via email) about events happening in WFBS. The events will either happen when the WFBS server triggers an alert or when the Agents or the MSA sends an alert to the server. Most of the alerts are easy to understand, and you should select that you want to get an email when the alert is triggered. A few of the less obvious alerts include:

Viruses detected on desktops/servers or Exchange server exceed: This is called an attack alert. If all of a sudden your users and/or your exchange server is detecting a large amount of viruses you should be alerted. You can choose how many viruses in how long of a time frame will alert you to. Now, selecting this option depends on how many users you have and how many email messages you get on a normal day. Overall a good choice is to select ten incidents in one hour on your desktops/servers and 100 incidents in one hour on your Exchange server. You can come back here and change it when you want to make it either more or less picky about alerting you.

Spyware detected on desktops/servers exceed: The same as the virus option, but you probably want to crank this up to be a bit pickier, upwards of five incidents per hour.

Network Virus: This is a very important alert and we actually recommend getting alerted as soon as this is triggered. To do so, you should select one incident in one minute.

	Device Access Control			
	ⓘ Device Access violations exceed:	☑	20 incidents within	1 hour(s)

Device Access Control: This alert will tell you when your users are abusing the device control policies. This is most useful because Trojans tend to also attack devices and you might be able to catch a problem using this notification. So we recommend you select 20 incidents in one hour.

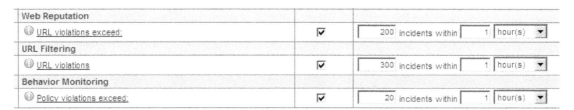

Web Reputation			
ⓘ URL violations exceed:	☑	200 incidents within	1 hour(s) ▼
URL Filtering			
ⓘ URL violations	☑	300 incidents within	1 hour(s) ▼
Behavior Monitoring			
ⓘ Policy violations exceed:	☑	20 incidents within	1 hour(s) ▼

Web Reputation, URL filtering and Behavior Monitoring: We have found that most people don't really want or need to be alerted to these triggers daily. Just getting a weekly report seems to be enough information for most administrators to handle any issues.

System Events

	Type	Email	Alert Threshold
⊟	Smart Scan		
	⊗ Smart Scan Service is not available	☑	
⊟	Component update		
	ⓘ Smart Scan Service not updated	☑	more than 24 hours
	⊗ Smart Scan Service not updated	☑	more than 72 hours
	⊗ Last console update time	☑	earlier than 14 days ago
	ⓘ Last console update time	☑	earlier than 7 days ago
	⊗ Update deployment rate after one hour	☑	less than 70 %
	ⓘ Update deployment rate after one hour	☑	less than 90 %
	⊗ At least one outdated Exchange server after deploying components more than 1 hour	☑	

System Events/Smart Scanning: These alerts will tell you when either your Smart Scanning Service goes offline (although it usually goes offline because the server itself is offline), or if the updates and deployments of the pattern files is delayed or not working.

Unusual system events		
⊗ The available free disk space is decreasing to less than:	☑	1 %

Free disk space: This alert will tell you when the hard drive that the WFBS server is installed on gets to within *X*% of filling up. We recommend setting this number to 5%, unless you are having free space problems.

License Events		
	Type	Email
−	License	
	ⓘ License expiration less than 60 days	☑
	⊗ License expiration	☑
	ⓘ Seat License usage is greater than 100%	☑
	⊗ Seat License usage is greater than 120%	☑

License Events: These events are automatically turned on and can't be turned off. We want to be able to remind you if your license is about to explore or your licensed seat count is over the licensed number.

Notification Settings:

Preferences > Notifications

Select the events that you want Security Server to notify you about. Click each link to modify the notification subject and

Events	Settings

Email Notification

From: Administrator@TrendMicroWFBS.Local

To: dale@jconsult.com

For example, user1@domain.com;user2@domain.com
(Separate multiple entries with a semicolon)

SNMP Notification Recipient

☐ Enable SNMP notifications ⓘ

IP Address:

Community:

Logging

☐ Write to Windows Event Log

The setup of the SMTP server itself will be explained later in this chapter. Here, you will decide who should be getting the notification emails.

From: Can be changed to any email address you like. If you want people to be able to reply to it, you will need to create a mailbox for the user you place here. The default name is *Administrator@TrendMicroWFBS.Local*

To: You can place what seems to be an endless list of email addresses in this box as long as you divide them by semicolons (;). If you use a mailing list, you can place that in here for easier administration of the names.

SNMP Notifications: If you utilize a SNMP monitoring program (And I doubt you do) you can set up the program to send a SNMP ping to your SNMP server.

Logging to Event Log:. If you want to also place these alerts into the Application Log, located on the WFBS Server event log, you can select it here. This is very useful if you want to keep a record of alerts that might help you or your server administrator to determine if something is going wrong on your server. **WARNING.** You do not want to send every alert set to a low threshold to the event log. It will quickly fill up the event log (or make it grow very large) and make it harder to use the event log.

Global Settings

Global settings apply to all computer(s) on the entire network.
You can export Global settings and other settings and later import into another installation

All Global Settings can be exported and imported between WFBS servers. This is useful as both a backup and a method of moving to another WFBS server.

Proxy Server

If you utilize a proxy server, you can set it here for the server to use. The proxy server will be used whenever the server connects to Trend Micro to get its updates.

Security Agent Proxy

Web Reputation, Behavior Monitoring, and Smart Scanning services use the pr
Provide logon credentials if the proxy server requires authentication.

☑ Use the credentials specified for the update proxy (above)

User name:

Password:

If you use a proxy server; Smart Scanning, Web Reputation, and Behavior Monitoring will need to talk securely to the server via the Agent. You can add the username and password for an account here. This will also allow for the Agent to get its updates for these products directly from Trend Micro.

SMTP

| Proxy | **SMTP** | Desktop/Server | System |

The following SMTP server settings apply to all notifications and reports generated by Security Server.

SMTP server: 2008-R2.vmware.jconsult.com

Port: 25

☐ Enable SMTP Server Authentication

User name:

Password:

Send Test Email

This is the SMTP server information used by the WFBS server to communicate notifications and send reports.

Desktop/Server

Default settings for all your Agents. These settings cannot be customized per group.

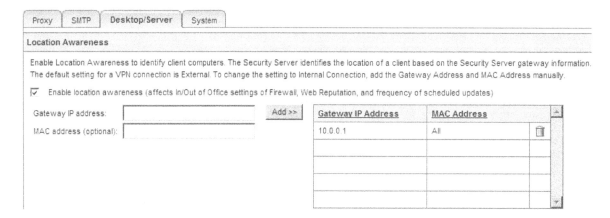

Location Awareness is used by Smart Scanning, Web Reputation, and Behavior Monitoring to determine which configuration you have set up in the Configure chapter.   The idea used here is to determine if the client can ping a gateway address on its segment.   If you open the IP properties on your network card settings you will see a default gateway listed.

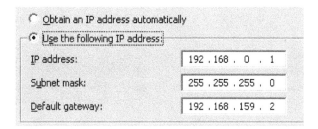

You will have to add at least one default gateway into your list. If your users in the office live on multiple segments (or you have more than one office), you can add more default gateways.

Once you have added your default gateways, the Agent will check to see if it can or can't ping the default gateway.   If it can ping the gateway, it will act with the *In the Office* settings. If it cannot ping the default gateway, it will act with the *Out of the Office* settings.

Help Desk Notice

The Help Desk Notice allows users to click on the Help Desk link on their Agent to contact your Help Desk or you directly. When clicked, an email message will appear addressed to what you have selected under *"Help Desk Email Address"*.   The *"Label"* you choose is what will be shown on the Agent, While the *"Addition Information"*, is what will appear when the user moves his mouse over the *"Help Desk: "* wording.

General Scan Settings

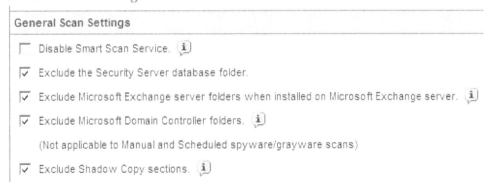

- **Disable Smart Scanning**: A discussion on Smart Scan is located in the Configuration Chapter.
- **Exclude the Security Server database folder:**   This will stop the Agent from scanning its own database. We have two feelings about this. First; scanning your own database is useless and could maybe possibly cause it harm (but we have never seen it happen). Second; however, not

scanning a whole folder is just writing a sign to a hacker saying "HEY PUT YOUR FILES HERE!" So we recommend you turn off this option, even though Trend Micro recommends leaving it on.

- **Exclude Microsoft Exchange server folders:** Like the last option, this does make us worry about security. *But* on a server, especially an exchange server, your security is much stricter and nothing is going to write into that folder except for the Exchange Server itself. So here we feel safe is excluding the Exchange Server folders that WFBS knows are really databases.

- **Exclude Microsoft Domain Controller folders:** On all AD servers, exclude the AD folders. Like Exchange folders we feel safe to exclude these files from scanning.

- **Exclude Shadow Copy selections:** There are some programs that make a live copy (shadow) of your data. We use this option to exclude these shadow copies from being scanned. We think this option should be selected and it is by default.

Virus Scan Settings

- **Configure Scan Settings for large compressed files.** The secret of understanding why this is an option has to do with the word large. Hackers tend to go for small, quiet, quick attacks on your computer. You won't see a hacker create a 500MB file for you to download, click on and run. At least we haven't seen it very often in the past. Scanning large compressed files is a large drain on the Agent. Because of the time and utilization wasted, WFBS has the option to stop scanning files over a certain size, and to only scan the first X number of files in any compressed file. We recommend not scanning any fie over 50MB and scanning the first 500 files in any compressed file. You can take the Trend Micro Default of 2MB and 100 files and you probably only see a little difference in speed.

- **Clean Compressed files:** This really means, "do I clean any files I find infected in a compressed file?" Although the chances of you being able to clean a file remain very low, there is no loss in giving it a try whenever the chance becomes available. We would select this option.

- **Scan OLE layers:** Object Linking & Embedding. This is when you take one type of file and embed it in another type of file. A good example is to embed an Excel graph inside of a Word document. The picture of the graph isn't placed in the document, a connection to the Excel document is placed in the file. So when something is changed in the Excel file, it is automatically changed In the Word file. So what if a Word document is embedded in an Excel file, then that

Excel file is embedded into another Word document. Each time a layer is added, the file that was embedded into the document must then also be scanned. So it is possible that over embedding can create a long delay as you open files. We recommend choosing 3 or 4 layers of scanning with this option turned on (as it is by default).

- **Add Manual Scan to windows shortcut menu:** This will add Manual Scan to the desktops or servers. When you click on a file or folder in your Windows Explorer or my computer, the option to scan that entry will appear as *Scan with Client/Server Security Agent.*

Spyware/Grayware scan Settings

Spyware/Grayware Scan Settings

☑ Add cookie detections to the Spyware log

- **Scan for cookies:** To scan for cookies or not to scan for cookies, that is the question. One problem we have is that WFBS considers every cookie that contains any data about you to be a bad cookie. This can be any data like your email address or name. But on the other side, there is no reason for a cookie to have any personal information. So although adding this option would be a good thing, on our own personal machines WFBS finds 15-20 cookies a day that it considers spyware. So we recommend using this option, but not adding them to the spyware log. That way you will have true spyware counted, not thousands of silly cookies.

Firewall Settings

Firewall Settings

☐ Disable Firewall and uninstall drivers ⓘ

- **Disable Firewall and uninstall drivers:** Overall most clients of WFBS use, and have no problems with, the firewall. If you are encountering network problems or slow times on your network, one of the things you can try to do is uninstall the firewall from the Agent. Sadly, this is only an option on all your machines and can't be done by groups. Uninstalling the firewall will completely uninstall it from each the Agents. If you want to add it back in, un-selecting this option will send the all the program files down to each agent and reinstall the firewall. The uninstall and reinstall will take some time for each Agent to do on the machines, and cause the Agents to restart.

Web Reputation and URL Filtering

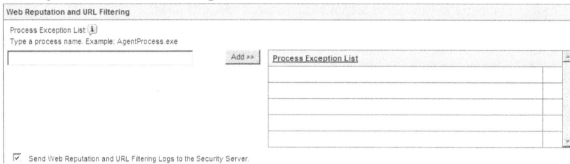

Trend Micro allows you to add approved processes into the Web Reputation and URL Filtering system used by the Agents (Check out the custom setup for groups to add approved websites).

- **Send Logs to Security Server:** This will have the Agents send a report of all of the URLs visited by the users on each machine to the server.

IM Content Filtering

This is kind of a silly addition to WFBS which gets you all excited when you first see it, but leaves you wondering why bother after you learn about it.   First, you can add a list of words or phrases that will not be allowed to be transmitted outwards in Instant Messaging programs.   The word will be replaced by a ***.   Now the problem is the user has to be running certain IM programs, this will not work with web-based IM or IM super programs like Trillian. Here is a list of programs that it will monitor; for the most part any of these IM programs built since 2008 can be monitored:

- Yahoo! Messenger
- Windows Messenger Live
- MSN Messenger
- ICQ
- AIM

Dale Johnson

Alert Settings

Alert Settings

☑ Show the alert icon on the Windows taskbar if the virus pattern file is not updated

after [7 ▼] day(s).

Select this if you want to automatically change the WFBS Agent icon on the workstation if the pattern file hasn't been updated in *X* amount of days. This is an excellent option to use and we recommend the 7 day default setting to tell your users that they need to update their client.

Agent Passwords

Security Agent Uninstallation Password

○ Allow the client user to uninstall Security Agent without a password.

◉ Require a password for the client user to uninstall Security Agent.

Password: [   ]

Confirm password: [   ]

Security Agent Program Exit and Unlock Password

○ Allow the client users to exit and unlock the Security Agent on their computer without a password.

◉ Require client users to enter a password to exit and unlock the Security Agent.

Password: [   ]

Confirm password: [   ]

Set the password that allows the user to either uninstall the Agent completely from their machine or simply stop the Agent from running on the workstation. We recommend using two separate passwords for these options and not using the same password you use for the WFBS server.

Preferred IP Address

Preferred IP Address

Clients with IPv4 and IPv6 addresses register to the server using [IPv6 first, then IPv4 ▼]

What IP system will the Agents talk to the Server, IPv4 or IPv6. The change will be obvious in the security Settings area where the Clients are listed. If an Agent does not have one or the other type of IP address, then the other will by default show up no matter what choice you choose here. When you make the change the server must communicate to the Agent to get the other address. The server does not hold or remember the other IP address.

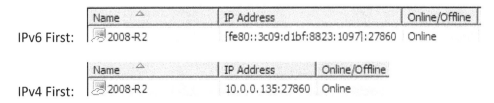

IPv6 First:

Name △	IP Address	Online/Offline
2008-R2	[fe80::3c09:d1bf:8823:1097]:27860	Online

IPv4 First:

Name △	IP Address	Online/Offline
2008-R2	10.0.0.135:27860	Online

Removing Inactive Agents from console

This will remove inactive clients from the console after *X* amount of days. This will remove either machines that have gone offline or machines that have left the office for more than x amount of days. You will need to turn this on if you have reached your number of licensed users limit and you want to clean up the consoles of older machines. You can also remove machines by hand in the Security Settings section. This does not remove the Agent from the machine; it just removes the Agent from the list of current machines. If the client comes back in they will appear again and take up a license. We find clients with a lot of Agents tend to use this option more than clients with a small amount of Agents.

Connection Verification

Connection Verification
☑ Enable scheduled verification
○ Hourly:
◉ Daily: Start time: 14 : 00 (hh:mm)
○ Weekly, every: Sunday
Verify Now

This allows you to check on the availability of all of the Agents that have been installed. If the client is not connected, they will appear as Offline `Offline` in the Security settings. We recommend doing this verification every day, or if you want to use it as a networking tool, you can even select once an hour. If you choose once an hour, it is best to pick a time of day when all users are connected to the network. If an Agent goes offline it will start it counter for the automatic removing of Agents from the Console we just talked about.

Quarantine Maintenance

Quarantine Maintenance

Specify the capacity of the quarantine folder and the maximum file size that Client/Server Security Agent can quarantine. These settings may affect the Security Server performance during a virus outbreak.

Quarantine directory:	C:\Program Files\Trend Micro\Security Server\PCCSRV\Virus
Total files quarantined:	0
Total files size:	0 bytes
Quarantine folder capacity:	10240 MB
Maximum size for a single file:	64 MB

Delete All Quarantined Files

In the Client Configuration Chapter, we determined what we wanted to do with clients we could not clean. If you choose Quarantine, this means the Agent would send the infected file (in encrypted form) to the WFBS server and it would be placed in the quarantine directory on the server. The default directory for the quarantine is: *C:\Program Files\Trend Micro\Security Server\PCCSRV\Virus.* On the Clients machine the files are kept in *C:\Program Files\Trend Micro\Client Server Security Agent\SUSPECT* until they are moved to the server. Neither of these directories can be changed.

- **Quarantine Capacity:** It is important that we choose a good size for the quarantine folder. By default it will fill up to 10GB worth of files. If you have the disk space and use quarantine this is a good number to keep it at. If you don't have the disk space or don't use quarantine, then we recommend brining that number down to a lower level. If the size of the folder goes over the limit, files will be deleted, starting with the oldest message, during the next system cleanup routine.
- **Maximum size for a single file:** Unless you routinely exchange large files, setting this between 50-75MB is a good idea. By default it is set at 64MB.

Security Agent Installation

Security Agent Installation

Security Agent Installation directory could be specified with the absolute folder path or the following variables:

$BOOTDISK: The drive letter of the boot disk
$WINDIR: The folder where Windows is installed
$ProgramFiles: The programs folder

Security Agent Installation directory: $ProgramFiles\Trend Micro\Security Agent

Here we can decide in what directory we will install the Agent on the workstations and servers. This will not change old installations or upgrades, only new installations from this point on.

Password Change

Preferences > Password

Set up the password for logging on to Trend Micro Worry-Free Business Security.

Old password:	
New password:	
Confirm password:	

Note: Passwords must be 1-24 characters.

Save

If you don't know your old password, check the Fixing Problems Chapter

Product License

Here, you will find your license information. You can *Enter a New Code* if you receive one from your reseller.

Refresh license information: When you renew your license keys, you will need to come here afterward (after you receive word from your reseller) and click on this link. This will check the license information and update your screen with the new renewal info.

Smart Protection Network:

Trend Micro uses this system to help determine what viruses are in the wild, where they are located around the globe and prepare emergency responses to attacks. You can also see this information at http://us.trendmicro.com/us/trendwatch. There is no real loss by saying yes; you will not be giving any data that will hurt your organization with this being enabled.

Chapter 8 Tools

WFBS gives you a few tools to make your administrative life a bit easier.

Administrative

Login Script Setup

2. **SETUPUSR.E**XE - If you use a domain this will place the install script into a user's Login script. The install process will then run when the user logs into the network.

   - **WARNING!!!** Running this program will delete your current Login Scripts!!!!! Do not run this unless you are sure it is safe.
   - If your users stay logged in overnight for long amounts of time, you will have to wait until they reboot or re-login to their machine.
   - The user must have administrative rights on the computer when they login.

   - The login script will work on the workstation that the user logs into, so you can do the install by hand. To do this, you need to have admin rights, install the script on your login, walk around and login to all the machines; each will get the program installed.
   - The user WILL SEE the install happen when they log into the domain. You might want to warn them if they are not used to things being installed without them knowing.
   - The login script will keep the OFCSCAN.BAT file in the user's profile until you delete it from profile.
   - It is recommended not to use this option on your servers.

   Once you make this selection, you will be given a help screen that simply sends you to run a program by hand to create the Login script. That program is

   *Program Files\ Security Server\PCCSRV\Admin\SetupUsr.e*XE

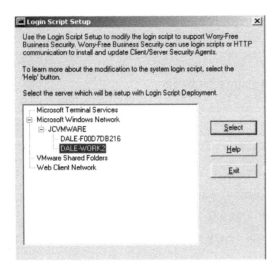

From the window, find the domain and server you want to add the login script to. You would usually select your domain controller here.

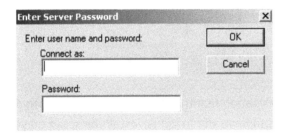

Type in the username and password to your domain using your domain name in the username like:

Jcinside\administrator

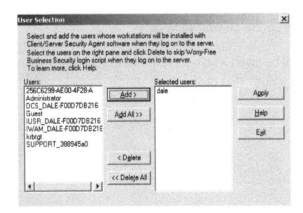

Select all of the users you want to add the login script to. Click on the Apply button and the script will be added to their login.

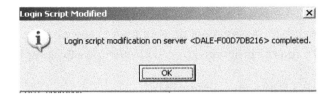

If you were to take a look at the user's profile you will notice that OFCSCAN.BAT is now added to their login script

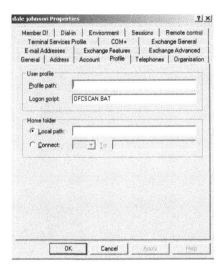

And the OFCSCAN.BAT file can be found in C:\WINDOWS\sysvol\domain\scripts on your domain controller. It should simply contain the command to run AutoPCC

\\SERVER_NAME\OFCSCAN\AUTOPCC

TMVS.EXE - You can go and actually run a Vulnerability Assessment on your own to see what it does or to see if something new is on your network. To run the program, go on your Windows Explorer to

C:\Program Files\Trend Micro\Security Server\PCCSRV\Admin\Utility\TMVS

and run *TVMS.EXE*.   TMVS is new in Version 8 and has less features than version 7. If you want more features go back to your old copy of the program.

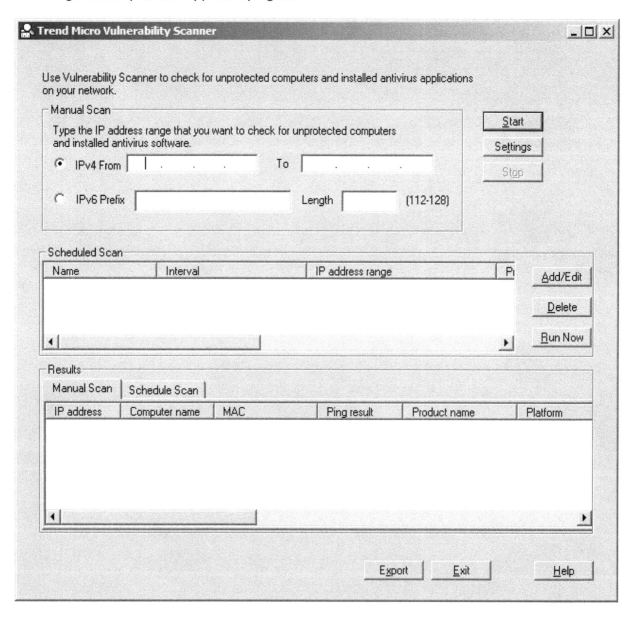

To run the program, you need to insert the range of IP addresses for the segment you want to check. So in the illustrated case, the network IP addresses are from 10.0.0.1 to 10.0.0.250. Click on the Start button after entering your IP address range and the program will go out and ping your network. You can watch the information on the bottom of the screen. A good way of checking the bottom without having to scroll is to click twice on the *Ping Result* | Ping result | column. This will sort all the computers the program found to the top of the list.

After finding the machines that are online, the program will then go to each address and complete an information check. Believe it or not; any program can ping any windows computer on a network and ask it pretty much anything about it. Microsoft calls this security. This is one reason why you had to buy WFBS. After a few minutes you will start to see the data for each computer fill out. You can use the bar at the bottom to go to the right and see all the data about all your computers that has been returned (this is only a small section of what was actually returned). Trend Micro will also return a result if McAfee or Symantec are located on the machines. It does not check for other anti-virus programs so if it returns that a machine has no anti-virus you will need to check to see if some other program is installed.

You can export this data for easier reading in a CSV file by clicking on the *Export* Button Export . You can now use this information to make sure all the machines currently on your network are up to your standards.

If you go into *Settings* Settings you can also automatically add the WFBS agent to all the computers you find without an anti-virus program.

Security Server settings (Specify a Server name or IP address)
dale-f00d7db216.jcvmware.local   Port: 8059
☐ Auto-install Client/Server Security Agent on unprotected computers.   Install Account...

The problem here is you need to have an administrative account name and password for the machine you are trying to install the Agent on. It's a nice thought, but if someone brings a computer onto your network, odds are you won't know that info.

But there is so much more TMVS does! Let's continue.

Scheduling Scans with Windows Scheduler

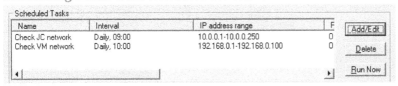

Scheduled Tasks
Name	Interval	IP address range	F
Check JC network	Daily, 09:00	10.0.0.1-10.0.0.250	0
Check VM network	Daily, 10:00	192.168.0.1-192.168.0.100	0

Add/Edit
Delete
Run Now

TMVS allows you to create schedules to check your segment (or other connected segments). Click on the *Add/Edit* button Add/Edit . You can then:

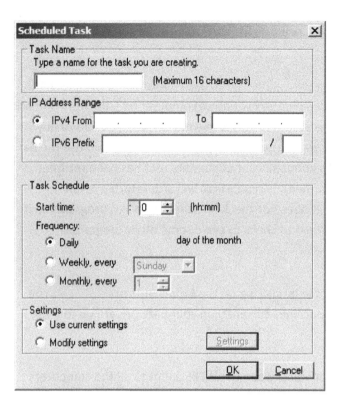

- Name your scheduled scan.
- Put in an IP range (This is great for checking numerous segments every day).
- A time of day to run (we recommend every day, during the morning).
- Utilize the current (or default) settings or make special settings for each search.

Run Now

Once you have created your searches you can wait for them to run or click on the *Run Now* button.

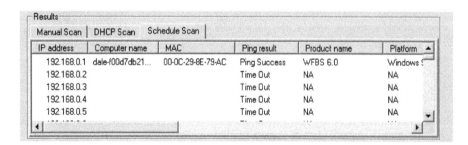

After a search runs, the data will appear under *the Schedule Scan* Tab. Only one search set of data will stay in the window at a time.

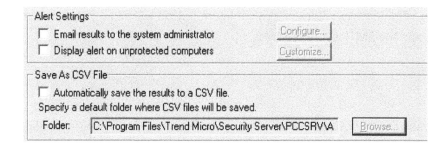

It is best to use the save as CSV options in the Settings (naming each scan a different file name) so that you can read the data offline. There are also an email option in the settings you may consider using.

Settings

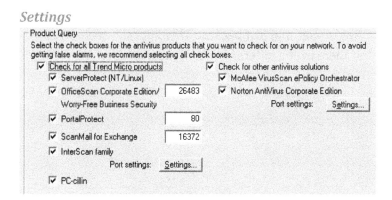

- **Check for all Trend Micro Products:** When doing a search, the search will give a positive response for all the products selected. We see no reason not to check all in this case.
- **Check for Other Antivirus Vendors:** TMVS will check for the newer versions of McAfee and Symantec. There is a hope that in the future other products will be placed in the product, but they haven't added any in the last 4-5 years.

- **Description Retrieval Settings:** This determines how deep TMVS will go when retrieving data during a scan. By default the scan is set to run a Quick retrieval. If you're doing scheduled scans and you have the time and computer utilization, we would recommend using Normal retrieval. You will get much more exact data and better checking of the data.

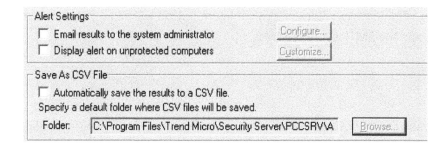

- **Email Results to the system administrator:** Clicking the configure button will allow you to select the From:, To:, the Subject, and the SMTP server address.

- **Display alert on unprotected computers**: An alert will be displayed on any computer that returns as not having anti-virus installed. Clicking the customize button will allow you to write out your own message for the alert. Remember that just because TMVS doesn't see a virus protection program, doesn't mean that there isn't a different one on the machine.

- **Save as a CSV File:** Allows you to create a CSV automatically whenever a scan is run (manual or scheduled). It is recommended that every scheduled scan have a different CSV name so they will not over-write each other.

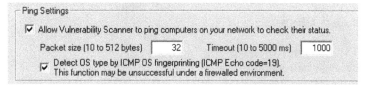

- **Ping Settings:** Only to be changed if you have a reason, but here you can change the size and timeout of the ping, along with the use of an ICMP echo request (Internet Control Message Protocol).

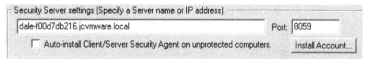

- **Security Server settings:** Here you can attempt to automatically try and install the Agent on machines that show that they do not have antivirus installed. The problem here is you will need the administrative account name and password for the machine you are trying to install the Agent on. It's a nice thought, but if someone brings a computer onto your network, odds are you won't know that info.

TMDISKCLEANUP.EXE - cleans up old files from your WFBS server. Run this file:

*C:\Program Files\Trend Micro\Security Server\PCCSRV\Admin\Utility\ TMDiskCleaner.e*XE

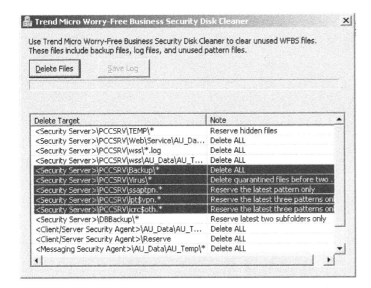

Select the files and types of files you want to clean up. When you click delete files, all of the unused files will be deleted. This means all old log files, pattern files and such items will be deleted (not entered in the Recycle Bin). This will affect any rollback operations and may affect log reports.   But, this will clear up disk space. A log file will be created upon completion which you can save.

If you run this program via the DOS Prompt you can throw on a few parameters.

/allowundo - place all deleted files in the Recycle Bin

/hide – hide the tool running (not sure why you would want to do this unless it was a routine command.

/log – if you hide you can also log the data into a log file.

You can even automate this tool to keep your disk space clean via Windows Scheduler.

- Go to Start -> Programs -> Accessories -> System Tools -> Scheduled Tasks

- Click on Add Scheduled Task.

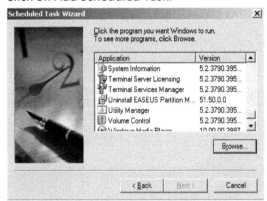

- This will start the wizard and after a few 'nexts' you will be asked to select the program to schedule. Click on browse and find:

*C:\Program Files\Trend Micro\Security Server\PCCSRV\Admin\Utility\ TMDiskCleaner.e*XE

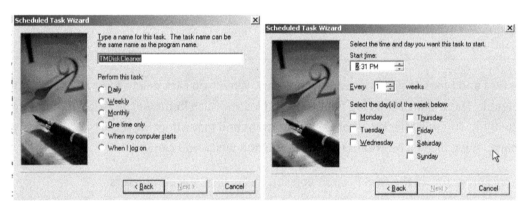

- Choose how often you want to run the program

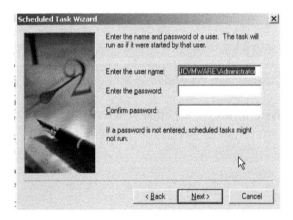

- You will need to include an account with rights to delete files on the server.
- Open the advanced properties on the finishing page.

- Add *"/hide /log"* at the end of the Run statement INSIDE the last quote. Your complete command should be:

*"C:\Program Files\Trend Micro\Security Server\PCCSRV\Admin\Utility\TMDiskCleaner.e*XE */hide /log"*

- Click Apply and Ok, and you should now see your schedule task listed on the scheduled page.

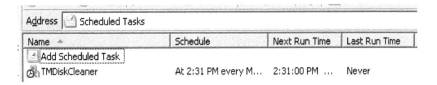

Remote Manager Agent
WFRMFORWFBS.EXE - Built for resellers/MSPs, this will allow them to monitor your WFBS and send you reports. Since it is for the Reseller we won't go into it here.

ScanServerDBMover.exe - Will allow you to move your database if the current drive that WFBS server is installed on is becoming too full or you want to move it to a different location on the same drive.

C:\Program Files (x86)\Trend Micro\Security Server\PCCSRV\Admin\Utility\ScanServerDBMover.exe

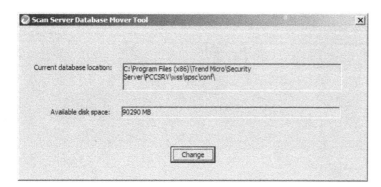

When run the program show the current location of WFBS database and how much space is still free on that drive. Clicking the 'Change' button allows you to now choose what drive you want the database to live on.

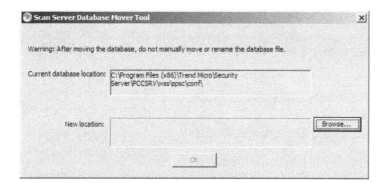

Clicking Ok will stop the WFBS services, move the database to the new location, and restart the WFBS services. **NOTE:** This process will take over control of the server during the move and your server may see an interruption. There is no backing out of the move half way through.

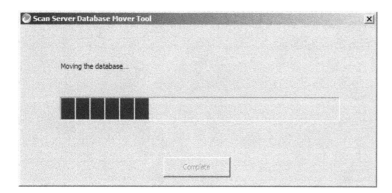

Clients

Client Packager

CLNPACK.EXE - This will allow you to create an actual executable (.exe or .msi) file to send to your users (via CD is best) so they can install the Agent straight to workstation.   After they are installed, the users will attempt to log back into the server, and when they do they will get any particular settings you have created for them.

- In windows explorer (on the server) go to
  Program Files\Trend Micro\Security Server\ PCCSRV\Admin\Utility\ClientPackager and run ***CLNPACK.e***XE.

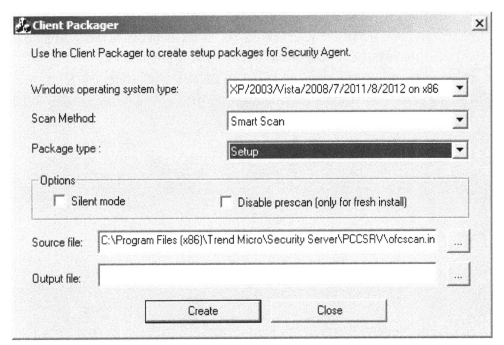

- **Target Operating System:**   Here, you need to select information about the client you will be installing the agent on. First, is the workstation a 32 bit (x86) or 64 bit (x64)?
- **Scan Method:** You can choose conventional scanning or smart scanning option for the workstation.   You must have the smart scanning option enabled on your server to have the option on your workstations. For more information on the difference see Chapter 7.
- **Package Type:** Are you installing the Agent as a new agent or upgrading from an old agent? It is recommended that if you are trying to upgrade old clients, you also create a new installation .exe along with your upgrade. If the upgrade fails the user will have to uninstall the Agent and reinstall it. You might as well get a step ahead and have it there with them to save you the headache when you get that phone call.
- **Options:**

- **Silent Mode:** The install is quiet and hidden from the user. Problem is you went through all this and have the user clicking on an .exe to start it. You might as well let them see something. If you want to hide it, hide it.
- **Disable Prescan:** Can only be chosen when you are installing the Agent as a new install. The option really makes no sense to choose unless you really have a short amount of time to do the install (or talk the user through it). It's always best to scan a workstation before installing an Agent.
- **Source File:**

  This is very important if you want to have the Agent you are installing connect to the server on a different IP address (like from the internet). If you have various IP or host name options you can create an .ini file for each. The quick way of making a change is to:
  - Make a copy of the OFCSCAN.INI in your server directory.
  - Find the *"Master_DomainName="* in the ini file. This should contain the IP address or domain name of your server. You can change this to the IP address or HOST name which your users will connect to your server with.
- **Output File:** Select a directory and name in which to call your outputted EXE or MSI file. The size of the output should be about 105-125MB.

VSENCODE.EXE - Allows you to unencrypt files once any Agent has found them suspect or quarantined. You can run this program on either the server or on an agent to unencrypt the files. **BEWARE: you are going to unencrypt a file that Trend Micro thinks is a virus. This is dangerous!!!! Also if you have not figured out why it was captured as a virus or you have not talked to Trend Micro about the file, odds are it will be encrypted again after you unencrypt it.**

Run this program at a DOS prompt with a –u parameter.

*C:\Program Files\Trend Micro\Security Server\PCCSRV\Admin\Utility\VSEncrypt\ VSEncode.e*XE *-u*

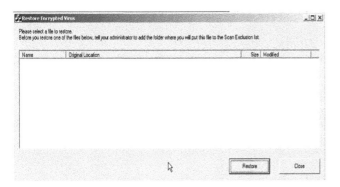

The default directory for the quarantine is*: C:\Program Files\Trend Micro\Security Server\PCCSRV\Virus.* On the Client's machines the files are kept in *C:\Program Files\Trend Micro\Client Server Security Agent\SUSPECT* until they are moved to the server.

A list of encrypted files will appear. You will need to know when the files were caught and maybe even an approximate size of the files you want to be unencrypted. Select the files and hit Restore. The files will show up in the original location. If they are still infected or WFBS thinks they are, they will once again be encrypted.

Log files are created by running this program, VSencrypt.log which tells you what it did with what files. There are more parameters and options available with this tool for the advanced manager. Check out the Administrator guide for those options.

IPXFER.EXE – This is a very useful tool that allows you to change which server that the Agent talks to. A few good examples of its use:

- You can use this tool if you changed the IP address or DNS name of the WFBS server.
- If your WFBS crashes and you created a new WFBS server on a different IP address or DNS name, this tool will point the Agents to that new information.
- If you have 2 WFBS servers, you can move users from one server to another.

C:\Program Files IPXFER is a DOS command tool. You need to either move it to the machine you want to use it on or find this file on your network. You will find it either on the server at:

*Trend Micro\Security Server\PCCSRV\Admin\Utility\IpXfer\ IpXfer.e*XE

Or over the network at:

*\\servername or ip address\ PCCSRV\Admin\Utility\IpXfer\ IpXfer.e*XE

In the DOS prompt on the machine whose Agent you would like to change, use this command after getting to the directory with IPXFER in it.

Ipxfer   -s [servername or ip address of new server] –p [listening port on new server] –m 1

Like   ipxfer –s dale-f00d7db216.jcvmware.local –p 8059 –m 1

The username and port are found on the new server under the Security Settings tab.

Ipxfer will then go and update the program with the new information. You can see if this has worked correctly with 3 methods.

- The new security server will see the transferred Agents appear under the security settings tab within the next 3 hours (the Agents check the server every 3 hours).
- Check the Help -> About -> More info in the Agent console, listed as Security Server name/port.

- Check the OFCSCAN.INI on the machine you changed and search for " *Master_Domain* "

  Master_DomainName=dale-f00d7db216.jcvmware.local
  Master_DomainPort=8059

REGENID.EXE – This tool will regenerate a new Agent GUID if either yours has become corrupted for if for some reason you can't get the Agent to show up on the System Console.

1. Copy C:\Program Files (x86)\Trend Micro\Security Server\PCCSRV\Admin\Utility\ WFBS_80_WIN_All_ReGenID.exe to the Agent computer.
2. Run the program, you will be asked to agree to the usual Licensing information and click the install button.
3. The program will stop your Agent, reset the GUID for the Agent, and restart it. Note sometimes it can take upwards of five minutes to fully take down the Agent.

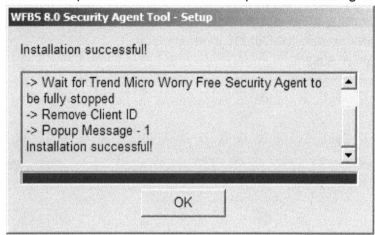

4. Now you must restart the machine.

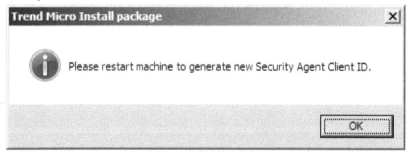

5. The next time the Agent calls the Server it will have the new GUID.
6. The old GUID and machine will still show in the Console until either it ages out (Enable automatically removal of inactive Agents) or you delete the Agent yourself. The system uses the GUID as the main sorting method.

Name	IP Address	Online/Offline
2008-R2	10.0.0.135:27860	Online
2008-R2	10.0.0.135:27860	Offline

SA_Uninstall.exe – This tool uninstall the Agent from the downstream for you.

First let's remember that you can uninstall the Client by deleting it from the Console. When you delete an Agent from the Console you will be asked if you want to also uninstall the Agent. If by chance you have agents that are not listed on the Console and need to be installed you can use this tool to uninstall the Agent.

1. Copy C:\Program Files (x86)\Trend Micro\Security Server\PCCSRV\Private\ SA_Uninstall.exe to the workstation you want to uninstall.
2. Run the program and it will unpack in the directory you select. Note the file will not clean itself up and it will leave those files on the machine. YOU WILL WANT to clean up after the program. You may also consider putting this unpacked program on the network out of the reach of the average user.

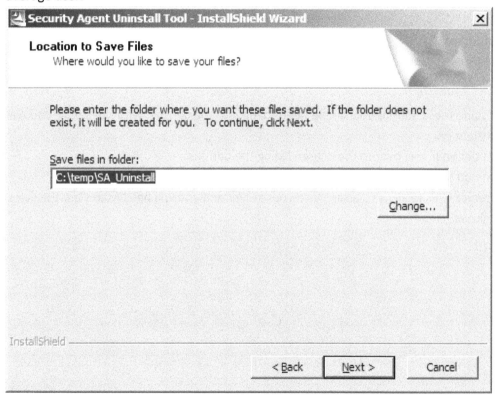

3. Go to the directory you have unpacked the files in and run the program **Unisntall.bat** under an account with Domain Admin privileges. You will also need to *'Run As Administrator'* if you are running the program on the desktop.
4. The program will turn off and uninstall the Agent.

```
C:\Windows\System32\cmd.exe
WFBS 8.0 Security Agent Uninstall Tool
Build 8.0.1200 Compiled on Wed 09/19/2012  2:50:10.20
Log file "Uninstall.12_29_02.log" is created.
```

5. Next the Workstation will need to be restarted.

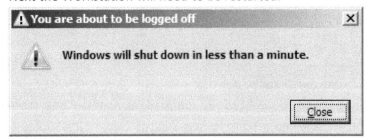

6. When you log back in you will need to install a new anti-virus program and clean up any files left over.

Add-ins

Live status Consoles

The following three add-ons can be placed on either your 2008 Essential Server, 2011/2012 Essentials Server, or your 2008/2011 Small Business Servers.

1. To include these add-ins you simple need to log into the console with the server you want to run the Add-in on.
2. Meander your way over to this screen listing the add-ins.
3. Download the Add-in to the server.
4. The server will install the package into your server and you will be able to view the live status on that server.

Chapter 9 The Agent

Let's take a look at how to use the Agent. A lot of options that the user can see in the Agent are customizable by you via the WFBS console. We will be looking at the Agent with all the options turned on, and note when options can be toggled on and off by the administrator.

You will be able to open the Agent console either by using the Start -> Programs

You can also open the Agent via right clicking on the Agent icon and selecting *Open Worry-Free Business Security*

The Agent Console

Status/Buttons

The front screen shows a few interesting pieces of information. This information is available for all your clients and cannot be turned off. If there is a problem with the Server or the License Key has expired a *"Protection at Risk"* message will appear at the top of the window.

- **Scan:** Will open up the *Scan and Clean* section new talk about later in this chapter.
- **Virus/Malware and Spyware/Grayware**: Shows how many problems have been found on the workstation in the last 24 hours.
- **Scheduled Scan**: The last scheduled scan that was completed (if it is enabled) and the time of the next scheduled scan.
- **Virus pattern:** Shows the current pattern file loaded into the Agent. It also shows the last and next time the client has contacted the WFBS Server (or last time they contacted Trend Micro if they are out of the office). Having 0.000.00 is a problem, if you see this number, click on the update button to the right. If after the update the number does not change, then you will need to figure out why the Agent is not communicating to the server or Trend Micro.
- **Update:** Update all your pattern files right now. If your Workstation is in the office and can see the WFBS Server it will get its updates from that server. If it cannot see the server it will go to Trend Micro to get it's updates. This is saying you didn't change the defaults in the server.
- **Language:** This version of the Agent allows the user to change the language seen by the icon and inside of the Agent program. Each change of language will close the Agent program and reset the language on the icon
- **Helpdesk:** This button allows your users to click on it and open up an email message addressed to your helpdesk. The message will contain a full list of information about the Agent itself.

- **Information Icon:** Sort of hidden, but the lower right icon when clicked on will produce a quick list of the Agent features and show which ones are on (green) and which ones are turned off (gray).

- **Unlocking the Agent:** Will allow the user to see and/or edit the features locked by the administrator in the console. The user will need to type in the administrative password, so this should only be used by the administrator.
- **All User Options:** Most of what the user can see beyond the main screen is defined via the WFBS console under Security Settings -> Configuration -> Client Privileges.

Logs

The Log screen allows the user to see any remaining logs (that have not been sent to the server) to look at what has happened on the Agent. The following logs are available:

- Virus/Malware
- Spyware/Grayware
- Firewall
- Web Reputation
- URL Filtering
- Behavior Monitoring
- Device Control

This is useful if you have users out of the office whom you are trying to diagnose with a problem.

- **Log Maintenance**: Will bring you to the Log Maintenance options in system settings. We will talk about that in a little bit.

The following system settings can for the most part be controlled by the administrator under Security Settings -> Configuration -> Client Privileges.   We will not go through each of these settings separately, you can see what they mean in the *Agent Configuration* Chapter.

Protection

This section allows you to Change the following settings, if permitted under Security Settings -> Configuration -> Client Privileges.

- Real Time Scan
- Manual Scan
- Schedule Scan
- Firewall
- Behavior Monitoring
- Trusted Programs

System

This section allows you to Change the following settings, if permitted under Security Settings -> Configuration -> Client Privileges.

- **Log Maintenance**: Allows the user to determine how long log files will remain on their systems. Do note that when the Agent talks to the WFBS server, it sends and deletes all of its log files. Therefore this option would only pertain to the Agent on machines that are out of range of their server.

- **Proxy:** This allows the users to change a proxy set between the workstation and the server. This is very dangerous to allow and should only be done in rare circumstances.

Notifications

This will allow the user to determine which Pop-ups the Agent places on the workstation when different problems are found.

Scan And Clean

Clicking on the Scan button will allow the users to scan their own drives manually. Once they click on the Scan button, a new window will appear showing the scan. This window cannot be closed or minimized and will take over control of the Agent program until the scan is complete, but you can pause or stop the scan. Once completed a rundown of the scan itself and any problems found will be listed.

- **Settings**: If enabled as a privilege will take you to the Manual Scan settings.

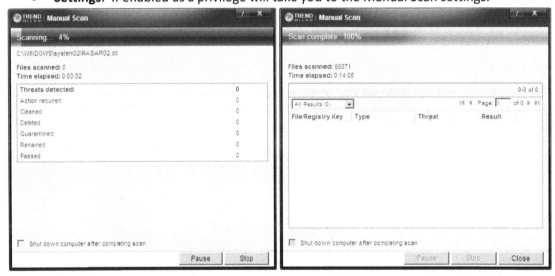

- **Shut Down computer after compeleting scan**: This is a very useful option if the user would like to run a scan at the end of the day and doesn't want to wait till the scan is done before leaving.

Scan Settings: The Scan Settings button will only appear if you enable the user to change the Manual Scan Settings in the console. Clicking that button will open up the settings window. We will not go through each of these settings separately, you can see what they mean in the *Agent Configuration* Chapter

Tools

On workstations (not servers), tools are used to help the user as they use the Internet. To do this, two toolbars are available for the user to install on their workstation. These toolbars do not load automatically; the user must load them.

- **Wi-Fi Advisor:** When enabled, this will allow the user to check the available wireless connections for security and encryption.
- **Trend Micro Anti-Spam Toolbar**: Once enabled, a toolbar will appear in the users email client and will allow them to choose whitelisted and blacklisted senders of email with use of their junk mail folder. The toolbar will work on Outlook 2003+, Outlook Express 6.0 SP2, and Windows Mail
- **Trend Micro Toolbar**:   Once enabled, this attaches to a user's browser. While the searching in Google, Bing or Yahoo, the user will get page ratings, telling them when pages are dangerous and shouldn't be clicked on.

- **HouseCall**: House call is the Trend Micro online virus scan that allows users to do an off-system scan of their workstations. This is very useful if the user thinks there is a problem with their system but yet WFBS does not see it. Also, some viruses attempt to stop the anti-virus program on the workstation, and you can use this option to delete the programs from the system. Clicking on the link will bring you to the HouseCall website (housecall.trendmicro.com)
- **Case Diagnostic Tool**: Clicking on this will bring you to the Trend Micro technote allowing you to download and run their diagnostic tools. Only do this if prompted by a Trend Micro support engineer.

Chapter 10 – Exchange

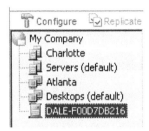

You can enter the Exchange configuration via the Security Settings section. Click on the Exchange server name and click on configure. In this version of WFBS you will not be able to go around and open the Exchange configuration separately.

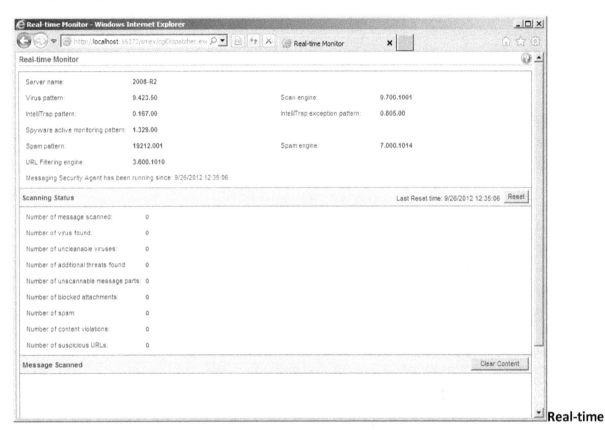

Real-time Monitor: MSA comes with a Real-time monitor that allows you to watch messages as they go through the server. You can get to this screen either by clicking on the Real-time monitor link Real-time monitor on the top of the MSA configuration or via the Start -> Programs selection.

Antivirus

The MSA (Messaging Security Agent) watches your Exchange server and scans messages as they:

- Enter the server
- Enter a mailbox
- Leave the server
- Enter Public Folders
- Move between Exchange servers

The MSA will do virus checking, spam detection, content filtering and attachment blocking.

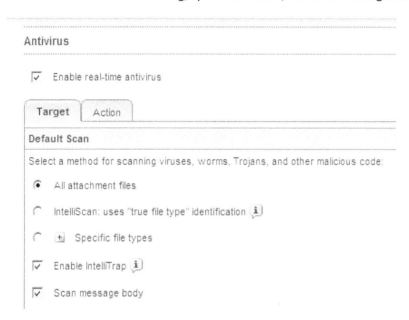

We need to choose which files to scan. All scannable files is the default.

- **All Scannable Files.** Simply put, if it can be scanned (it's not encrypted in some way) we will scan it, every time it moves, is opened, is saved. Everything all the time.
- **IntelliScan.** Instead of looking at the file extensions (.bat, .exe, .doc….)while scanning, we will look inside the file header to figure out what it the file really is. This is set as the Default setting and unless you have a reason should remain so.

  Inside IntelliScan

  Not every file is as it seems. Every file has an extension. This enables Windows to determine what program should run the program. .doc files are for a word processor. .exe files are executables. But anyone can change these extensions and therefore break how Windows start a program. How/Why? Maybe you have worked for a company that didn't let you email pictures. To get around it you could simply rename the file from .jpg to .abc. The email system is only looking for picture file extension .jpg; since .abc isn't blocked it lets the file go. In the email you tell the person on the other end to change the extension back to .jpg to use it. IntelliScan looks inside of every file it scans for the header, which tells the WFBS more about the file than just what an extension is. In the header, you will see stuff like what kind of file it is, when it was created, how big it should be…. IntelliScan allows you to stop your users from breaking the system by changing extensions, and more importantly, stops hackers from hiding bad programs behind the mask of a simple and boring file extension.

- **Specific file types**. Here we will look at only the file extensions to determine if a file should be virus checked. If you select this option, you can edit the data inside the box to add or subtract extensions. We do not recommend this option unless you really, really have a good reason.

After you think you have a good reason, you should then call someone to talk you out of it.

- **Enable IntelliTrap:** : One way of hiding a virus is to compress it numerous times into a file. This can be an effective hack because your antivirus software is set to ignore compressed files over *X* amount of compressions. This is set on by default.

    In less nerdy terms, if I take an EXE program and compress it into a Zip file, it really doesn't do anything but it does change the file extension to .zip and now the header is a zip file. So the EXE is hidden behind the zip file and can only be found if the EXE is opened. Now WFBS will check inside the zip file and look at the EXE file to virus check it. But let's now keep zipping the zip file, say 14 times. If so; your computer looks at the zip file and sees:

.zip -> .zip -> .zip -> .zip -> .zip -> .zip -> .zip -> .zip -> .zip -> .zip -> .zip -> .zip -> .zip -> .exe

    Now some virus protection programs (this one included) will allow you to choose how many levels of that zip file (or any compressed file) to look into before giving up. If you hide it deep enough, the virus protection will give up!

    IntelliTrap allows the WFBS to look into the compressed file, look real deep (20 layers or so), and check to see if anything is hiding. Different compression programs have different rules about levels of compression. IntelliTrap has a database of compressions types and is better than you at trying to figure it out.

- **Scan Message Body:** : Email messages can contain MIME based embedded data. For this reason, it is possible that a virus could be in the body of a message. We should always leave this option turned on.

Additional Threat Scans

Additional Threat Scan

☐ Select All

☑ Spyware	☑ Adware
☐ Dialers	☐ Joke Programs
☐ Hacking Tools	☐ Remote Access Tools
☐ Password Cracking Applications	☐ Others

This option is offering to stop other bad types of emails. By default, the system has only selected Spyware and Adware. We think it would be smart to select all of these expect for Others, which really is a bit of a tossup. Exactly what are these options?

- **Spyware:** Programs that install on your computer capture data (usually key strokes) and send the data to a server somewhere in the world to be abused. Some of these are also known as Keyloggers.
- **Dialers:** Not used much these days, but before broad-band we all used to connect to the internet with a modem. To do this the modem needed a dialer. Some enterprising people figured out if they could make you use their dialer, they could charge you some ridiculous cost per minute to connect to the internet.
- **Hacking Tools:** The name pretty much says it. If a hacker can get a hacker tool on your computer, they can hack it.
- **Password Cracking Applications:** Replaced mostly by more powerful keyloggers, these programs would attempt to figure out your system passwords.
- **Adware:** Programs that put advertisements pretty much everywhere on your computer. These started soon after the beginning of the internet and will never go away.
- **Joke Programs:** These programs usually don't do real harm (but they have been known to occasionally), but they tend to scare the user into thinking something is wrong with their computer, their car, or the world.
- **Remote Access Tools:** Programs that once installed by a hacker will allow them to take your computer over remotely. Very dangerous.
- **Others:** Other programs and bad things defined by Trend Micro.

Exclusions

Exclusions

Do not scan attachment and/or message body if:

☑ Message body size exceeds:	30	MB
☑ Attachment size exceeds:	30	MB

Do not scan compressed files if:

☑ Decompressed file count exceeds:	9999	(1-10000)
☑ Size of decompressed file exceeds:	100	MB
☑ Number of layers of compression exceeds:	5	(1-20)
☑ Size of decompressed file is "x" times the size of compressed file:	1000	(100-1000000)

You can also stop messages from entering the Exchange server by defining limits to the message. Administrators used to limit message and attachments sizes more often when hard drive space was expensive to buy and maintain. In these days of Terabyte drives for under $100, these options are used less. But if your server has free space problems you may consider using them. These are turned on by default, you can turn them off by un-clicking them.

- **Message body size exceeds:** This option will stop any message with a message body over X amount of size from being accepted into the server. It is not normal for a message body to be of that size or contain that many embedded parts. Default is 30MB
- **Attachment size exceeds:** This will stop any message with a combined attachment size over X amount of size from being accepted into the server. If you routinely send large files , then you will need to turn off this option. Default is 30MB
- **Compressed file scanning:** The secret of understanding why this is an option has to do with the word large. Hackers tend to go for small, quiet, quick attacks on your computer. Over email they can make the attack a little bigger without you noticing. Scanning large compressed files is a large drain on the MSA. Because of the time and utilization wasted, MSA has the option to stop scanning files over a certain size, and to only scan so many layers of the compressed file.
- **Decompressed file count exceeds:** This will not scan a compressed file (let it proceed) if there are more than X amount of files contained in the file. Default is 9999, which is probably a bit high. Maybe 5000 is a good number.
- **Size of decompressed file exceeds:** This will work if, after uncompressing (decompressing happens after diving in the ocean) the files, one of the files exceeds X MB in size. This is a weird setting (not just the name of it). One large file in a compressed file will let the rest of the compressed file through. That seems like an easy way for hackers to go around the system. Default is 100MB, we recommend turning this option off.
- **Number of layers of compression exceeds:** Now you have to consider how much computer time and utilization it takes to unzip a zip file 20 times to find that .exe file. It takes a lot. So here we are going to limit the layers of compression to check for normal compressed files that IntelliTrap has already OK'd or ignored because it doesn't see a problem. Want to move it up to 6? Go for it. 20? That will cause the message to really slow down the system. Default is 5; we think 5-6 is a good number to use.

- **Size of decompressed files is "*X*" times the size of compressed files:** If a file expands *X* amount of times when it is uncompressed, then it didn't really contain much information in the first place. Again this is a good way for a hacker to get around the system and we recommend it be turned off. Default is 1000.

Antivirus Actions

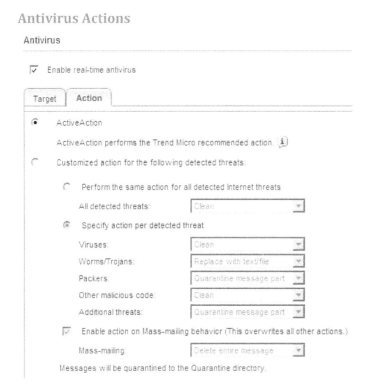

- **ActiveAction: :** In the Actions tab, you will tell WFBS what to do when it encounters a problem. The default setting (letting WFBS decide) is by far the best choice. In the last several years, viruses have become un-cleanable. Back in the 1990's viruses would try to infect a single file. Those files were sometimes cleanable, and you could actually use the file after cleaning the virus out of it. As Virus writers have progressed, they no longer look into infecting single files, but have progressed into infecting your process DLLs and EXEs. So Trend Micro has developed a system that determines by each infection type how to deal with the files infected. These change daily and we highly recommend using Trend Micro's ActiveAction decisions.
- **Customized Attacks:** Here, you can choose how you want to handle infections when the system finds them. Let's look at the different threats:
  - **Viruses**: Any file found trying to infect your system or a file.
  - **Worms//Trojans**: These are attacks on your system. Instead of just infecting your system, these lovelies will install programs on your system and run processes in the background. Sometimes you will know something is wrong, sometimes it will hide and gather data.
  - **Packers**: A packer is a method of getting worms, Trojans or root kits onto your system. The idea is to hide the EXE that starts the infection inside of compression files.

- o **Other malicious code**: Assorted programs that will do something bad to your system.
- o **Additional threats:** Additional problems listed in Trend Micro's database.
- o **Mass-mailing behavior:** Not as used as it once was, the idea is to infect your Microsoft Outlook program so that it will send out mass mailings of spam to your contact list. Getting the spam message to be sent from you to someone you know, allows the spammer to get a better chance of it being read. Mass mailings can contain more than words, including things like Trojans and worms.
- **Customized Actions:** Now, let's look at the different things you can do to any message that is found infected. Note that email messages are handled differently than desktop viruses because Microsoft Exchange has certain demands on the anti-virus program.
  - o **Clean:** Clean the infection and follow the "Do this when clean is unsuccessful"

    Do this when clean is unsuccessful: | Delete entire message ▾ | selection lower on the screen.
  - o **Replace with text/file**: If an attachment is found infected, delete it and replace it with a text file. The message will then be sent along with the fake attachment. The information in the text file is customized further down the page.
  - o **Quarantine entire message:** This will automatically send the message along with attachments into quarantine. The user will not receive any notification of quarantine.
  - o **Delete entire message:** Deletes the entire message, with no notification.
  - o **Pass**: Let the message go (not something we recommend).
  - o **Quarantine the message part:** Sends the infected attachment to quarantine, but sends the rest of the message along with no note of the

    Do this when clean is unsuccessful: | Delete entire message ▾ |

    ☐ Backup infected file before performing action

    ☑ Do not clean infected compressed files to optimize performance. ⓘ

    deletion.
- **Do this when clean is unsuccessful:** Choose what to do when you selected either:
  - o Clean as an option above
  - o ActiveAction.

  We recommend choosing Replace *with text/file* or *Quarantine the message part.*

- **Backup infected file before performing action**: This is a safety that will back up the file before taking the infected attachment apart for cleaning. If you have problems with clean files being corrupted, you should turn this option on. If you're deleting or replacing infected attachments, it won't do anything turned on. You can elect what directory to back the files up to further down the page. It is not selected by default.
- **Do not clean infected compressed files to optimize performance**: This option looks at the attachment; if it is a compressed file of some type it will simply delete the attachment and send the message along. This option is selected by default and although it makes sense not to spend all that time trying to scan a compressed file, if your users do send compressed files back and forth it may be a bad option to turn on.

```
Notification

┌ Notify recipients ▾

    ┌ Do not notify external recipients

┌ Notify senders ▾

    ┌ Do not notify external senders

    ☑ Disable sender notifications for spoofing emails
```

Whom do you want to notify that a virus was found and dealt with?

- Notify recipients: This sends a note to all recipients listed on the message (To, CC, and BCC) is sent.   Most people turn this option on; it is off by default.
- Do not notify external recipients: If recipients do not have a mailbox on the server, do not send them a message.   The scenario in which you would use this is if your internal users are sending out viruses, you probably do not want to let your customers know you're infected.   This is not selected by default.
- Notify Senders: This will notify the senders of a message they are infected.   Some administrators like to do this; some don't bother.   We recommend you turn this on if your customer base sends lots of attachments to your users. It is not selected by default.
- Do not notify external senders: As just explained, we recommend this on if you have large attachments coming from your customers. This is not selected by default.
- Disable sender notifications for spoofing emails: A spoofing email is when the person named in the "from" of the message is not the actual person who sent it. It is easy for an email program (or spammer) to change the from address to anything they want.   MSA can verify if a message is spoofing one of its own users. How? Well if the message says it was created by you and it wasn't created by the exchange server, then it must be spoofed.

Macros

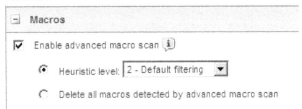

Attaching viruses into Documents via the use of macros is a very effective way of getting abusive programs onto a workstation. We should enable this option, as it is by default.

- **Heuristic Level:** This looks dead into the macro, defines what the macro is going to do and chooses if this falls within certain levels which we can select. The leveling is set from lenient filtering to Rigorous filtering. The higher the filtering level the more time will be taken to tear apart the macro and the stricter the filter will be in deciding if the macro is bad. The default is set to 2 (Default filtering) and is recommend to stay at this level unless you have had problems either not catching or catching too many macro viruses.
- **Delete all macros by advanced macro scan:** If a macro is found, the macro is deleted. This is pretty hard stuff as most people use macros effectively day to day. This is not selected by default and unless you have a severe problem, should not be.

Unscannable Message Parts

What happens when you get an attachment that is either encrypted or password protected? Since there is no way for this file to be virus checked, most administrators would just pass it along. If you use encrypted mail, then you must pass the files. We recommend pass as the choice, unless you're being infected by password protected files.

Excluded Message Parts

Excluded Message Parts	
Files over specified scanning restrictions:	Pass

What do you do with attachments that were found to be too big or have too many compressed files as seen earlier on this page? Most administrators would pass the attachments as they simply don't expect very large attachments to be infected. You could quarantine the attachments if you think that there could be a problem and you will want to get to the attachment if it is actually good. By default, the setting is set to Pass.

Dale Johnson

Backup Setting

If you have chosen earlier to backup files before cleaning them, we can select here where we would like to place those encrypted files. By default the directory is set to:

C:\Program Files\Trend Micro\Messaging Security Agent\storage\backup

Replacement Settings

Type the text or file name that replaces the infected content when you select the **Replace with text/file** action or **Quarantine message part** action

Replacement file name: VIRUS_DETECTED_AND_REMOVED.TXT

Replacement text: The Messaging Security Agent detected and removed a virus from the original mail entity. You can safely save or delete this replacement attachment.

If you have selected at any time to replace an attachment with a Text/File or chosen ActiveAction, you can customize the message that is put in that replace text file. When the user gets the message and sees the attachment (named VIRUS_DETECTED_AND_REMOVED.TXT), they can open it and see the text typed in here.

Anti-Spam

Spam is found by two methods; Email Reputation and Content Filtering.   Email Reputation uses Trend Micro's reputation database to determine if the sender of the message is accurate, while Content Filtering looks for words in the email message to determine its value.

We recommend that you stop your spam before it gets into your Exchange server using either an Email gateway or a messaging cloud service. Why?   Exchange is a server hog; always has been and always will be. The more mail that attempts or enters the exchange server takes more server utilization (and therefore more hardware) to handle it. Even if it's deleted by the spam program, the server still had to spend a lot of time dealing with it.   If we delete it before it even gets to the exchange server we are both using a program meant to stop spam (exchange is meant to send mail not stop it), and we are keeping our exchange server smaller and more nimble.

> *Inside Exchange SMTP and SPAM: What is SMTP on an exchange server? SMTP is the Simple Mail Transfer Protocol and developed in the 1970's to enable two different users on two different servers on the pre-Internet to send basic text messages between each other. It grew in the 1980s and 1990s to include Attachments (MIME) and even included in the late 1990s an implementation with security (which has pretty much failed to be implemented). The whole idea of SMTP mail was a simple fast way to send mail between two servers. No security, no worrying about who sent it or who is receiving it, just get an email from point A to point B.   This was such a fabulous way of sending because we trusted everyone back then, to a point that if I was sitting at home and had to send a mail message to say Microsoft, I could make a connection with Apple's mail server and it would help me send it. Then came the spammers. They figured out " this is a free way of sending out our advertising, our cost is really cheap, just a machine to send it, and everyone else will suck in the costs of sending the mail for us." Well at first spam was real advertising (the first real spam started around 1994), but then it started to slowly get the attention of scammers and the messages started to spam fake messages trying to make money for fake items. In the late 1990's we started to turn off our open SMTP systems and you could no longer use Apple to send a message to Microsoft.   In the last 10 years, SMTP systems have become tighter, spammers have become 90+% of the mail on the Internet, and we have to all buy these programs to stop it.*

Email Reputation
Email Reputation (via the Exchange SMTP)

☑ Enable real-time anti-spam (Email Reputation)

> *Inside Exchange SMTP: how mail is received: SMTP is a process on your Exchange server that listens on Port 20 for calls from other machines sending SMTP messages. Once a machine contacts your SMTP server a session is created. The SMTP server then has a few pieces of information including the IP address of the sending machine. Email Reputation is working with Exchange SMTP at this level to deny connections and stop the session before any message information is received into exchange. Once the connection is accepted, a bunch of commands are interchanged between the sending machine and the exchange sever and the message's attachment are sent to the server. The following works differently on the various versions of exchange server, but the main idea is that once received the files are kept like a text file on the server until the Exchange server takes the message and places them into the Exchange server for delivery. The step of accepting the message for delivery is where the MSA does all its content and virus checking of the files. So although the email has been accepted it has not entered the Exchange database when the processes are run. Passed messages are placed in their correct mailbox or sent to the correct mail server (if the person lives on a different Exchange server).*

Once enabled, MSA will use two services levels to determine how you want to determine if an email message is spam. Each one of these options will stop the message at the SMTP interface and not allow it into the exchange server at all.

DO NOT enable this option if you use a spam filter before your Exchange server.

- **Standard**: Trend Micro maintains a RBL (Real-time Blackhole List) of IP addresses. These IP addresses have been gathered over the years and contain IP addresses that have been known to send spam messages.   The positive of using this list is if you know an IP address sends spam you don't want to get mail from it. The negative is that IP addresses change often on the Internet, and some of these may have gone from bad spammers to good businesses. Trend Micro doesn't monitor the RBL list for addresses that have returned to a good state. Overall we do recommend using Standard as you will probably not encounter an IP address that has gone from Bad to Good. There is a method below for white listing (approving) IP addresses if you do run across a problem.

- **Advanced**: Uses the same database as Standard, plus adds a dynamic database that maintains a list of recently known spam IP address. This is a better way of stopping spam. If you get a few spam messages from the same IP, tell the MTA part of exchange to stop accepting spam from that IP address for *X* amount of time. If the MTA continues to receive mail from the IP address, continue to keep the name on the bad list. If by chance the MTA stops sending mail, give it a while and take it off the list. We would rather see the whole system work like this worldwide, but it is a good method for stopping spam. We recommend starting with Standard and working towards Advanced if you see a continuing spam problem.

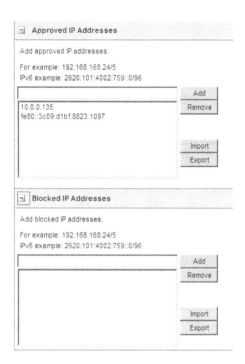

- **Approved/Blocked IP address.** Here, you can over-ride the Email reputation settings and add your own IP addresses that you either approve or want to block. A note about approving addresses: Lots of companies have more than one outbound mail sending server. Many of these companies do not use the same outbound mail servers as they do inbound mail servers, so you cannot look up a company's MX record to determine the IP addresses of the servers. Therefore you can block IPs by groups. If you contact a company and they say "all our mail servers are from 10.0.0.1 to 10.0.0.15," you can simply add one entry to say 10.0.0.1/14. Over all if you have a problem receiving mail from a company you should contact their IT department to get their list of approved SMTP server IP addresses.

If you want to Block/Approve email addresses or domains you can do that at the next step, content filtering.

Service Portal: Email Reputation Service is an add-on that allows you to filter inbound mail before it gets to your Exchange server. Contact your Reseller on adding this option to your setup.

Anti-spam Content Scanning

In content scanning, we will attempt to determine if a message is spam by the content of the message itself.

Anti-spam Scanning Filtering Target

- **Spam detection level:** The MSA will use its Spam pattern file with defined words to filter, assign them heuristic rules and values and depending on your level selection will decide to pass or stop the message. The quick look of how heuristics work is to look at the message like a human does. If certain words, certain expression, certain ways of display words, look weird or don't follow correct rules of communication, we add 1 to our starting score of 0. We keep doing this throughout the whole message adding up our score until we finish with the message. By selecting a level, you will have pre-chosen a score that will automatically call that message spam.
    - **Low**: This level of spam is saying "I pretty much only want to stop spam if it's obviously spam." With this setting you will rarely get a false positive (A good message that gets stopped by spam). But you will see spam messages in your users' mailboxes.
    - **Medium**: Now you are picking up the score a bit and saying "ok, I want less spam and I don't mind an occasional false positive."
    - **High**: WE DON'T WANT SPAM. We don't really care about false positives, stop it ALL!!!!!!!

The best method of determining your spam level (and it seems everyone has a different one) is to start at the lowest level, use it for a week. Determine if the spam you are getting is too large; if it is try the next level up for a week. Your users will tell you if they are missing messages and getting too much spam (You don't have to worry about that), so make sure they are part of the testing.

- **Detect Phishing**:. A phishing email is an email that attempts to get a user to log into a fake website and gather their information (username password or something worse). These are easy to determine because the coding of the message hides the true site identity from the user. Actual code in the message would look like this.

`<a href="http://www.badsite.com/get data.htm"> http://www.jconsult.com/login.htm </a>`

The average user will simply click on the message and start entering data into someone else's database.

MSA will check the message for known phishing methods and stop it.

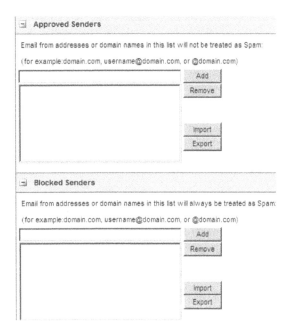

- **Approved/Blockers Senders**: Here, you can add email addresses or domains that will be automatically deleted or passed by the content filtering systems. If you attempt to block spam by blocking email address and domains you are never going to win the battle. Spammers change their From: information constantly in messages. Do not go down the road of trying to chase spam by using this as a device.

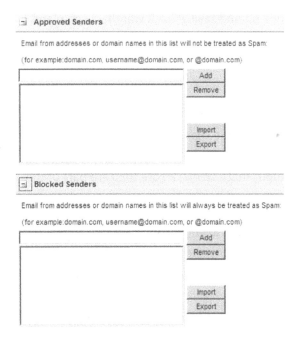

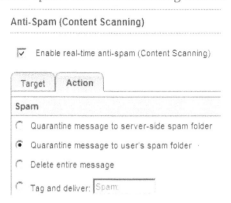

- **Spam**: What do you want to do with the messages once content filtering determines it is spam? We recommend either Quarantine option.
    - **Quarantine the message to the server side spam folder: this w**ill send the message onto the server.   The message will stay there until it is deleted by maintenance, and you can view it with the quarantine tool further down this chapter.   The user will not know the message has been quarantined.
    - **Quarantine the message to the users spam folder: This will s**end the message into the user's mailbox but place it into the spam folder. If the IMF (intelligent message filter) is installed on the server, this will send the message to the assigned user's spam folder.
    - **Delete entire message:** This simply deletes it from the server.
    - **Tag and Deliver:** Add this to the "from" of the Subject line and send the message to the inbox. An example of a message before and after:
        - **Before:** *Take a look at this new mailbox*
        - **After:** *SPAM: Take a look at this new mailbox*

- **Phishing Incident**: What do you want to do with the messages once phishing determines it is a bad message?   We recommend the Quarantine or delete option.
    - **Quarantine the message to the server side spam folder:** Will send the message onto the server.   The message will stay there until it is deleted by maintenance and you can view it with the quarantine tool further down this chapter.   The user will not know the message has been quarantined.
    - **Delete entire message:** This simply deletes it from the server.
    - **Tag and Deliver:** Add this to the "from" of the Subject line and send the message to the inbox. An example of a message before and after:
        - **Before:** *Update your bank info*
        - **After:** *PHISHING: Update your bank info*

Content Filtering

In content filtering, we look at the insides of the message; where is it from, what does it say, what is attached and determine if we are going to stop the message.

- **Enable content filtering**: Turn this module on or off.
- **Adding a new Filter** Add . Not for the average person, but if you want to add a filter you can create a list of definitions to check the message with. You can use this filter to either add to the blocking rules or use it to define messages you know are good. If you are going to do this, we recommend you enjoy the WFBS manual on how to do it. We will only gloss over these options in this book.

- **Filter Type**: You can choose what type of filter you want to use.

You will have a list of conditions; if any are found then you need to trigger this message to do what you want. This is good for finding information that can be in any message.

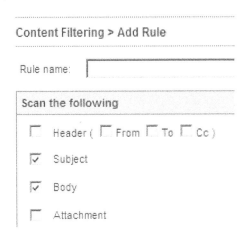

- Choose which parts of the message to search

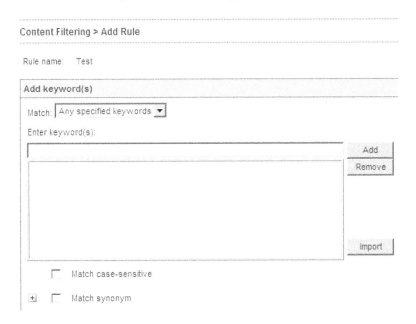

- Chose the words to add, if they should be case sensitive, and list any synonyms you may want to also add. Next we decide what you are going to do with these messages, including:

Content Filtering > Add Rule

Rule name: Test

Select an action

- ○ Replace with text/file
- ● Quarantine entire message ⓘ
- ○ Quarantine message part
- ○ Delete entire message
- ○ Archive

Notification

- [+] ☐ Notify recipients
- [+] ☐ Notify senders

- Replacing the message with a default message you can create yourself
- Quarantining or deleting the message
- Archiving the message into a directory and delivering the message as normal (This is called spying)
- Along with action you performed to the message, notifying either the sender or recipient a message saying you performed the action.

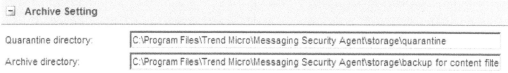

⊟ **Archive Setting**

Quarantine directory: `C:\Program Files\Trend Micro\Messaging Security Agent\storage\quarantine`

Archive directory: `C:\Program Files\Trend Micro\Messaging Security Agent\storage\backup for content filte`

Archive Settings: You can change where the messages and their attachments will be archived during this process. This allows you to have different locations for different blocks and allow different people to see the different archives. Note HR.

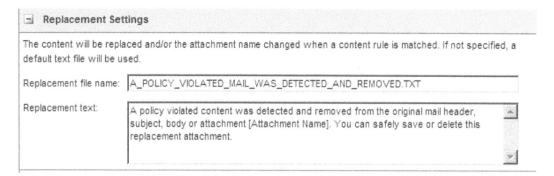

⊟ **Replacement Settings**

The content will be replaced and/or the attachment name changed when a content rule is matched. If not specified, a default text file will be used.

Replacement file name: `A_POLICY_VIOLATED_MAIL_WAS_DETECTED_AND_REMOVED.TXT`

Replacement text: `A policy violated content was detected and removed from the original mail header, subject, body or attachment [Attachment Name]. You can safely save or delete this replacement attachment.`

Replacement Settings: You can also create a file that has will replace the blocked attachment and call it and put in it what you want. In Exchange any attachment that is blocked must be replaced with another file.

Dale Johnson

Filter messages that match all conditions defined

You will have a list of conditions that you want to trigger if they are all found. This is good for finding a particular message.

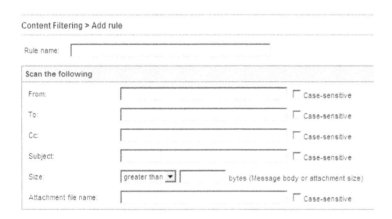

Here, you need to decide what data you want to search for. Again all these much match to trigger the rule.

Decide what you are going to do with these messages, including:

- Replacing the message with a default message you can create yourself.
- Quarantining or deleting the message
- Archiving the message into a directory and delivering the message as normal (This is called spying)
- Along with action you performed to the message, notifying either the sender or recipient a message saying you performed the action.

Quarantine directory: C:\Program Files\Trend Micro\Messaging Security Agent\storage\quarantine

Archive directory: C:\Program Files\Trend Micro\Messaging Security Agent\storage\backup for content filte

Archive Settings: You can change where the messages and their attachments will be archived during this process. This allows you to have different locations for different blocks and allow different people to see the different archives. Note HR.

□ **Replacement Settings**

The content will be replaced and/or the attachment name changed when a content rule is matched. If not specified, a default text file will be used.

Replacement file name: A_POLICY_VIOLATED_MAIL_WAS_DETECTED_AND_REMOVED.TXT

Replacement text: A policy violated content was detected and removed from the original mail header, subject, body or attachment [Attachment Name]. You can safely save or delete this replacement attachment.

Replacement Settings: You can also create a file that has will replace the blocked attachment and call it and put in it what you want. In Exchange any attachment that is blocked must be replaced with another file.

Monitor the message content of particular email account(s)

Here, we are going to look for an email address in either the From:, To: or CC: of the message.

Content Filtering > Add Rule

Rule name:

Add email account(s)

From:

To:

Cc:

What email addresses do you want to search for and in what part of the message? Adding "Joe" to all the parts means you are watching for all of Joe's emails.

Content Filtering > Add Rule

Rule name: test

Scan the following

☑ Subject

☑ Body

☐ Attachment

Add keyword(s)

Match: Any specified keywords ▼

Enter keyword(s):

[   ]   Add

[   ]   Remove

                                  Import

☐ Match case-sensitive

± ☐ Match synonym

Are you going to search the message for any particular words?   We do **NOT** have the ability to not scan for words, we have to do some content scanning here.

Content Filtering > Add Rule

Rule name: Test

Select an action

○ Replace with text/file

◉ Quarantine entire message ⓘ

○ Quarantine message part

○ Delete entire message

○ Archive

Notification

± ☐ Notify recipients

± ☐ Notify senders

- Replacing the message with a default message you can create yourself
- Quarantining or deleting the message
- Archiving the message into a directory and delivering the message as normal (This is called spying)
- Along with action you performed to the message, notifying either the sender or recipient a message saying you performed the action.

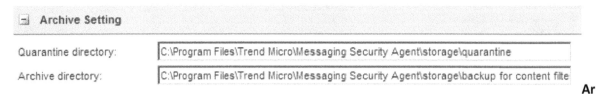

Ar

chive Settings: You can change where the messages and their attachments will be archived during this process. This allows you to have different locations for different blocks and allow different people to see the different archives.   Note HR.

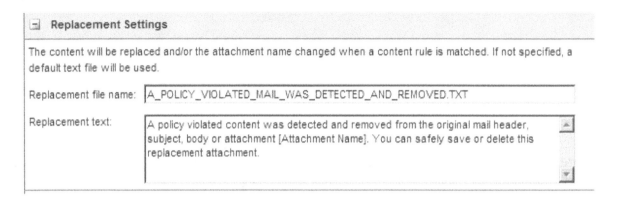

Replacement Settings: You can also create a file that has will replace the blocked attachment and call it and put in it what you want. In Exchange any attachment that is blocked must be replaced with another file.

Create an exception list for email account(s)

Here, you can create a list of people who you don't want any email they receive or sent dealt with by the content filters.

Content Filtering > Add Rule

Rule name: Stooges in Sales

Messaging Security Agent does not apply content rules with a lower priority than this accounts in this list

Specify an email account list exception rule:

	Add
Curly@jconsult.com	Remove
Larry@jconsult.com	
Moe@jconsult.com	
	Import

List the users you want in this rule. When you are done, you should reorder this rule to Number 1 so it runs before all the other rules.

An excellent rule to use is called the Golden Word. The idea is to have a special word, which, if placed in the subject line, will allow the message to skip all content filtering and go right to the user's mailbox. This is useful for management or salespeople who always have that "It must get to me" type of emails. Let's create it:

- Create a Filter **messages that match all conditions defined** Rule.

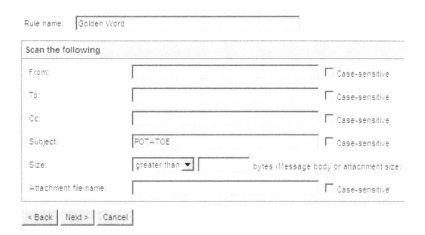

In the subject line, put your secret word. I tend to use a misspelled word so that there is less of a chance it will be passed by accident.

Choose Pass entire message, And finally, reorder this rule to number 1

Data Loss Prevention

Data Loss Prevention is the ability to watch email messages for data that you don't want to be sent out of the building. There are other versions of DLP available via Trend Micro if you are interested in a version that does more things.

To do this, you have some pieces of the program you will need to configure. Let's take an overview and then dive deep into setting it up. First, a few notes:

- DLP can be assigned to turned on or off for everyone in your server. You cannot decide who uses and doesn't use it.
- You can choose what level of blocking, from archiving a copy of the message to quarantining to replacing the email.
- DLP will not search password-protected or encrypted files.

Keywords: Keywords is basically content filtering of the email. Looking for specific words, words that are like a specific word, or groups of words put together with other words in a specific way.

An Example would be to look for words used in Perl scripting.

Expressions: Indentifiers are the specific data we are looking for.

An Example would be an Identifier that looks for a Social Security Number (SSN).

Enable real-time Data Loss Prevention: Will turn on DLP and monitor the about bound stream for any rules that are enabled.

Dale Johnson

Rules

DLP is actually controlled by the Rules you create and turn on. Trend Micro has given us a few default Policies to use and learn from.

- **Download more default Rules**: This will allow you to download more current rules from Trend Micro. At the writing of this book the rules only contained rules you would use in other countries besides the US. Each of these rules can be imported using the 'Import' Button

  Import.

  DLP - APAC

  DLP - Canada

  DLP - France

  DLP - German

  DLP - Ireland

  DLP - Other European

  DLP - Spain

  DLP - United Kingdom

- **Status:** The status shows you if the Policies are turned on or off. If you click on the status of a Policy it will change the status to the opposite (Off ⊖ or On ⊙).

- **Action:** Describes what action the rule will take if it finds a message that matches its rule.

- **[A-Z]+:** By mousing over the magnifying glass you can see what the expression for that rule is set at.

  American Express card number 🔍   Quarantine entire message

  ,REG. \b3[4,7]\d{2}\-?\x20?\d{6}\-?\x20?\d{5}\b

- **Reorder:** It is important that the rules are ordered correctly. You do not want rules deleting or removing messages before another important rule reads them. Selecting the rule and clicking the 'Reorder' Button allows us to change the priority of that rule. We can only reorder rules one at a time. It is VER YIMPORTANT that after you reorder the rules you click on the 'Save Reorder' Button Save Reorder at the bottom of the list. We will put money on you missing this a dozen or so times like we have.

  ☑ Visa Card card number 🔍   Quarantine entire message   1 1   ⊙

Click the *'Add'* Button ☐ Add to create a new Rule.

Data Loss Prevention > Add Rule

Scan the following

☐ Header (☐ From ☐ To ☐ Cc)

☑ Subject

☑ Body

☐ Attachment

Add keyword(s)

Enter a specific **keyword**, Regular Expression, or use an **example** to generate Regular Expression.

⦿ Keyword

  Keyword: _____

○ Regular expression (auto-generated) ⓘ

○ Regular expression (user-defined)

Scan the Following: Where are we going to search for in the email messages for the data that might trigger a Template. There are certain reason to look at the Header information compared to the Subject, Body and Attachments. Usually this has to do with what exactly we are looking for. If this policy is to look for certain words, then we might consider looking for them in the Header. If it's to look for something like a SSN, then there is very little chance you will find on in the Header information.

Add Keywords/Expressions: Here we are going to add the Keyowrd or expression we want to search for:

- **Keyword**: Type is the word you are exactly looking for. You can use any of the following types of characters. You can find some excellent training on the use of Logical Operators and Regular Expressions on the Internet:
    o Words:
    o Numbers:
    o (&*@)(*@$
    o Short phrases: like 'great book'
    o Logical operators: .AND. .OR.
    o Regular Expressions .REG.
- **Regular Expression (auto generated)**: Regular expressions are used to match certain types of strings of characters. Examples are a Credit Card Number or a Social Security Number. Auto

generated means the server will build an expressions for you. Simply give the Rule a name and give an example of what the rule looks like. The program will come out with a Regualr Expression to use.

⊙ Regular expression (auto-generated) ⓘ

Rule Name: ISBN

Example: 894-0302213-874   (40 characters limit)

| 8 | 9 | 4 | - | 0 | 3 | 0 | 2 | 2 | 1 | 3 | - | 8 | 7 | 4 |

☐ Constants   ☐ Variables

Regular Expression:
.REG. \b[0-9]{3}\-[0-9]{7}\-[0-9]{3}\b

Provide another example: If you have two examples it would be best to use them to help determine if the expression is correct.

☑ Provide another example to verify the rule (Optional)

089-932hg94-634   [Test] ✕

- **Regular Expression (user defined)**: Regular expressions are used to match certain types of strings of characters. Examples are a Credit Card Number or a Social Security Number. User defined means you have done your homework and know exactly what the expression is.

⊙ Regular expression (user-defined)

Rule Name: ISBN

Regular Expression: .REG. \b[0-9]{3}\-[0-9]{7}\-[0-9]{3}\b

Provide another example: If you have two examples it would be best to use them to help determine if the expression is correct.

☑ Provide another example to verify the rule (Optional)

089-932hg94-634   [Test] ✕

Select an Action:

- **Action Settings**: What are we going to do when we trigger off a template in our Policy?
    - **Replace with text/file**: If an attachment is found by a template, delete it and replace it with a text file. The message will then be sent along with the fake attachment. The information in the text file can be customized further down the page. You cannot replace an attachment at the Transport Layer as Exchange demands that the message at this point stay as one piece.
    - **Quarantine entire message:** This will automatically send the message, along with any attachments, into quarantine. The user will not receive any notification of quarantine.
    - **Quarantine Message Part:** This will automatically send the message part that was found by a template, into quarantine. The user will not receive any notification of quarantine. Finding the information in the Header or Subject will send the whole message to quarantine UNLESS it's found in the Transport Layer (In that case it isn't quarantined at all)
    - **Delete entire message:** Deletes the entire message, with no notification.
    - **Archive**: Sends the Message along but also sends a copy to the Archive Directory, logging or notifying you about the event.
- **Notification:** If we selected to notify in the last screen, we can here determine how and who to notify.
    - **Notify Sender**: Tell the sender that they have done something wrong.
    - **Do not send to External senders:** Never send a message to an external user, they don't work for you anyways.

        ☐ Do not notify external sender(s)

    - **Notify Recipients**: Tell the recipient that they are receiving a message that has triggered the rule.
    - **Do not send to External senders:** Never send a message to an external user, they don't work for you anyways.

        ☐ Do not notify external sender(s)

- **Advanced Options**

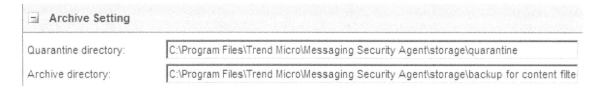

    - **Backup Directory**: By default, the directory is set to:
      C:\Program Files\Trend Micro\Messaging Security Agent\storage\backup for content filter
    - **Quarantine Directory**: By default the directory is set to:
      C:\Program Files\Trend Micro\Messaging Security Agent\storage\quarantine

Dale Johnson

- o **Replacement Settings:** If you have selected to replace an attachment with a Text/File you can customize the message that is put in to replace the text file. When the user gets the message and sees the attachment (named A_DLP_POLICY_INCIDENT_WAS_DETECTED_AND_REMOVED.TXT), they can open it and see the text you typed in here.

Domains

The domains listed here will not be filtered by DLP.

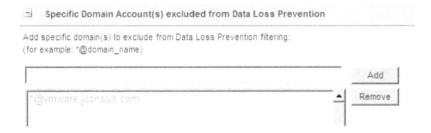

Approved Senders

The email addresses added here will not be filtered by DLP.

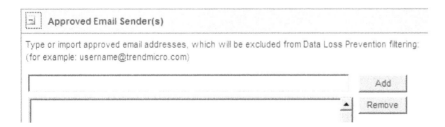

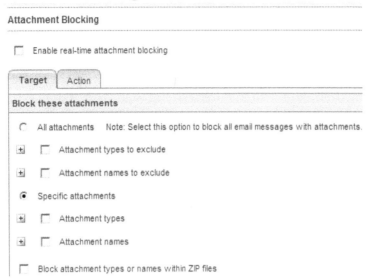

- **Enable real-time attachment blocking:** Turn on or off the Attachment blocking module.
- **All Attachments:** Do you really want to stop all attachments?

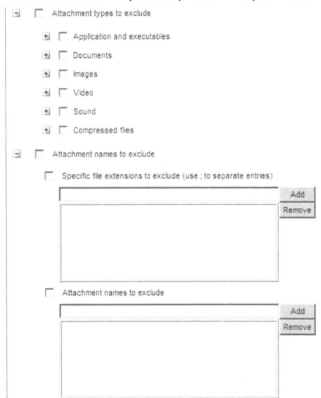

OK. Well, then you can select which types, extensions or file names to allow through even though you are blocking all other attachments.

- **Specific Attachments**:

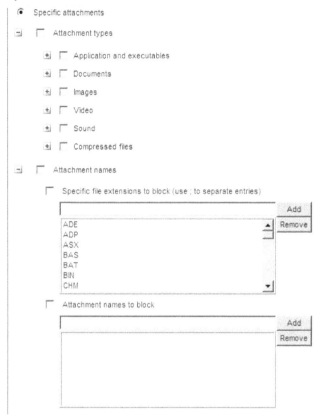

You can select what types, extensions (a bunch are already setup and turned on for you) or file names to block.

- **Block attachment types or names within ZIP files**: Do you want to also block attachments that fit your criteria inside of ZIP files?

What are you going to do with these messages? You have options, including:

- Replacing the message with a default message you can create yourself.
- Quarantining the attachment, quarantining the entire message or deleting the message
- Along with what you're doing with the message, notifying either the sender or recipient a message saying you did it.

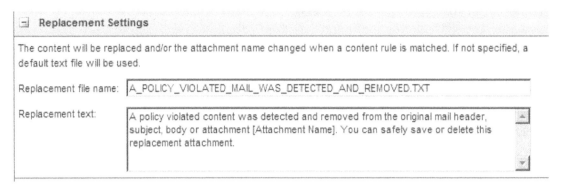

Replacement Settings: You can also create a file that has will replace the blocked attachment and call it and put in it what you want. In Exchange any attachment that is blocked must be replaced with another file.

Web Reputation

Web Reputation uses the Trend Micro Web Reputation Database to scan each email for the appearance of bad web page links (URLs) via content control.

Target

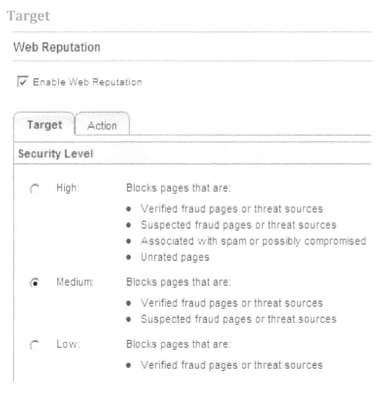

- **Enabling Web Reputation**: will start the content control of web links.
- **Security Level**: How aggressive do you want to be at blocking bad web links? Medium is the default and is probably the best selection to start with.

Trend Micro maintains a database of websites that it considers to have reputations (bad ones for this purpose) about. They have divided those sites up for WFBS in the following categories:

- **Verified fraud pages or threat sources:** These are known web sites and pages that have a virus, spyware, or such attached to them. If you go there, you will have a problem.
- **Suspected fraud pages or threat sources:** These sites have been found to have problems, but have a lower rating as either the problems with the site aren't full time or some people consider the threat ok (like a screensaver program). It is probably best to try this setting and see if your users complain about not going to these sites.
- **Associated with spam or possibly compromised:** These sites are from known spammers or maybe have been compromised due to the web system they are running. Certain types of websites are less secure then others; these sites are in the very unsecure zone and either can be or have been compromised.   Choosing this will block some sites your users might

actually use. Sadly, lots of websites are ignored by their webmasters. They have been left alone or the webmasters don't care to secure them.

- **Unrated pages:** These are mostly new pages that simply haven't been rated. A webpage needs to be searched or used by Trend Micro's clients and its internal servers before it gets a rating. You would probably not want to use this option for your users; the web grows so many pages a day, and your users will come across new pages often enough to make this a bit annoying.

Can you see the pages listed in these groups? No. Trend Micro keeps the database secure so that the hackers that make these sites won't know that they have been found. You can search individual web sites using their reclassification tool at: http://reclassify.wrs.trendmicro.com/ to check for issues. You can also tell Trend Micro about websites you either want to add to the database or sites you want them to take off the database. This webpage can only be used by administrators and will make you put in your license key to secure that only Trend Micro clients are doing updates.

- **Approved URL List:** Adding a URL here will both allow that direct link to be allowed in all emails, but all pages under that URL will also be added. An example: Allowing *www.jconsult.com* will also automatically allow *www.jconsult.com/insidewfbs* and any other *www.jconsult.com* page.
- **Import/Export:** You can use a file to import or export lists of files between systems.

Web Reputation

☑ Enable Web Reputation

Target	Action

Specify action

⦿ Quarantine message to user's spam folder

○ Delete entire message

○ Tag and deliver : | Suspicious URL: |

☐ Take action on URLs that have not been assessed by Trend Micro ⓘ

AND

○ Notify

⦿ Do not Notify

Notification

[+] ☐ Notify recipients

[+] ☐ Notify senders

What can you do when the program finds a bad URL in a message? Note that the MSA cannot change an email message, it can only change its location.   So when you choose an action, the bad URL which instigated the action will still be in the email message after it is moved.   We recommend either quarantining or tagging these messages as an action.

- Quarantine to spam folder: Will send the message into the spam folder in the user's mailbox.
- Delete entire message: Doesn't trust any message with a bad URL, so deletes them all.
- Tag and deliver: Changes the subject line of the message to start with the information places in the box. By default the box contains Suspicious URL
- Notifications: Do you want to notify people that a bad URL is being sent around?   About the only reason you might want to do this is to inform your users when they send bad URLs out. If you want to use this feature, then select *Notify senders* and *Do not notify external users* (There is no reason to send Bad URL information to the spammers on the Internet who sent them In the first place).

Quarantine

Quarantine Query

This will allow you to look into the server quarantine and bring up messages, and resend the message to wherever it was expected to go in the first place.

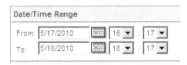

- **Date/Time Range**: Select when you think the message you are looking for was sent. By default, you only hold 30 days' worth of messages.

- **Reason Quarantined**: If you know when the message was quarantined and you want to reduce the output, you can select the exact reason for the quarantine. If you don't know the answer you can select All reasons.

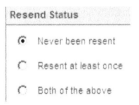

- Resend Status: Do you know if the message has already been resent out of quarantine? Selecting Both of the above is a good option.

Advanced Criteria
Sender:
Recipient:
Subject:
Sort by: Scan time ▼ ○ Ascending ● Descending
Display: 15 per page

- **Advanced Criteria**: What information will define the message you are looking for? You can choose how many messages to display on the page at once and you can sort by:
  - Scan Time
  - Reasons
  - Sender
  - Recipient
  - Subject
  - Filename
  - Quarantine path
  - Resent Status

Once you have clicked on the *Search Button* Search , you will have a listing of messages found. If you find the message you want to resend, you can click on it and hit the resend button. It will skip the checking and go directly to the recipients listed in the message.   You cannot see what's in the message unless you resend it to the recipient and go read it.   When you resend a message copy of it will remain in the quarantine.

Quarantine Maintenance

Most administrators find over time that the quarantine becomes less used as when you first installed WFBS. Users will become used to the deletion rate of spam and hopefully, you will configure the exceptions to eliminate the use of the quarantine.   Over time, we tend to see either the quarantine being turned off (just deleting everything) or the amount of days to keep messages drastically reduced from 30.

Manual Maintenance

Last quarantine maintenance: Not available

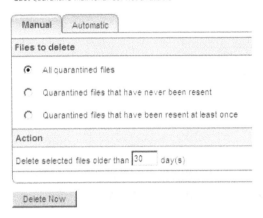

Here, you can automatically clean up your quarantine directory and get rid of old messages.   By default, the message will be deleted after 30 days (We can set this in a few seconds). When you delete messages older than *X* amount of days, you have the options to choose:

- **All quarantined files**: Deletes all the messages located in all the quarantined directories.   This is a great way of getting some disk space back.
- **Quarantined files that have never been resent**: Only deletes messages that have spent their whole lives in the quarantine and nobody has come to claim them.
- **Quarantined files that have been resent at least once**: Only deletes messages that have been queried and resent to their recipients.

Automatic Maintenance

Last quarantine maintenance: Not available

| Manual | Automatic |

☑ Enable automatic maintenance

Files to delete

- ◉ All quarantined files
- ◯ Quarantined files that have never been resent
- ◯ Quarantined files that have been resent at least once

Action

Delete selected files older than 30 day(s)

Save   Restore Defaults

You can turn off and on the automatic deletion of messages in the quarantine directories. This will both keep the database quick and easy to search and save some disk space.   Your options here are deleting message over *X* amount (30 days is the default) old including:

Dale Johnson

- **All quarantined files**: Deletes all the messages located in all the quarantined directories. This is a great way of having some disk space left.
- **Quarantined files that have never been resent**: Only deletes messages that have spent their whole lives in the quarantine and nobody has come to claim them.
- **Quarantined files that have been resent at least once**: Only deletes messages that have been queried and resent to their recipients.

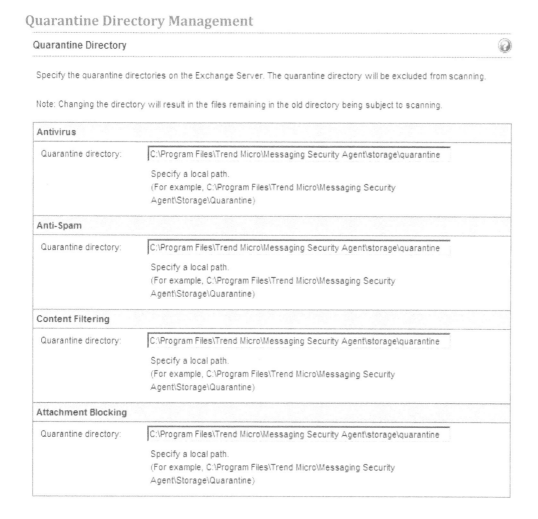

Here, you can move the different directories where you place messages entering quarantine. Default settings for all the directories are:

C:\Program Files\Trend Micro\Messaging Security Agent\storage\quarantine

If you quarantine a good deal of messages or you do a lot of queries, you may consider placing the messages into different directories to speed up your queries.

While you were working with the different settings in the MSA, you may have set up notification messages to send to users. Here, you can decide how to handle those messages a bit.

- **Administrator Account**: Here, you can choose the From: of each message sent out. You can either make this a fake address so it cannot be replied to, or you can make this a real email address that can be replied to and dealt with.
- **Internal Email Definition**: Who do you consider internal email users? As we made our setup, you had the option to select *Do not notify external recipients*

☐ Do not notify external recipients

Here, you can decide between:

- **Default (Internal mail: email messages with the same domain.):** The person must be in the same domain to be considered internal.
- **Custom internal mail definition**: You can add your own domains names or exact email addresses to consider internal. This is useful if your company uses lots of email addresses and domains.

Operations - Trend Micro Support/Debugger

This section can be used when Trend Micro Support requests that you enable log files to fix problems that you can't resolve.

Support/System Debugger

	Module Description	Module Name	File Name
☐	Trend Micro Messaging Security Agent Master Service	<SMEX_Master.exe>	SMEX_Master.log, SMEX_Master-yy-mm-dd-xxxxx.log
☐	Trend Micro Messaging Security Agent Remote Configuration Server	<SMEX_RemoteConfig.exe>	SMEX_RemoteConfig.log, SMEX_RemoteConfig-yy-mm-dd-xxxxx.log
☐	Trend Micro Messaging Security Agent System Watcher	<SMEX_SystemWatcher.exe>	SMEX_SystemWatcher.log, SMEX_SystemWatcher-yy-mm-dd-xxxxx.log
☐	Virus Scan API (VSAPI)	<store.exe>	store.log, store-yy-mm-dd-xxxxx.log
☐	Transport Service	<edgetransport.exe>	edgetransport.log, edgetrans-yy-mm-dd-xxxxx.log
☐	Common Gateway Interface (CGI)	<cgiDispatcher.exe>	cgiDispatcher.log, cgiDispatcher-yy-mm-dd-xxxxx.log

To turn the log type on and off, you need to select or deselect the type of log. These log files will grow fast and big. We do not recommend using this option on your own or for a long time. Also, the log files will remain there until you delete them. If you create a log file for Trend Micro, don't forget to delete it after you send it.

Chapter 11 – Plugins

Plug-in Manager

To start using Plug-ins, you must first download the Plug-in Manager in Preferences -> Plug-ins

Preferences > Plug-Ins

Plug-in Manager

With Plug-in Manager, you no longer need to wait for a product release to start using server and client plug-in programs. Plug-in Manager displays these programs in this screen as soon as they become available.

Read the following instructions carefully before installing Plug-in Manager:

1. Plug-in Manager cannot be installed remotely. Open the web console on the computer where Worry-Free Business Security is installed and then install Plug-in Manager from there.
2. Other requirements:
   - At least 200 MB available disk space.
   - You must have an internet connection to download the Plug-in Manager installation package from Trend Micro. If the computer has no internet connection, contact your administrator for assistance in setting up a local update source.

[Download Plug-in Manager]

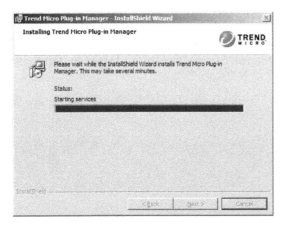

- Once the Plug-in Manager is installed, a list of available Plug-ins will be shown. At the writing of this book, only Security for Mac was available.

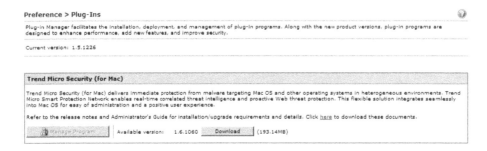

- Clicking on the *Download* button will start the download.

Trend Micro Security (for Mac) Download

Downloading Trend Micro Security (for Mac) version 1.6.1060, please wait. You may navigate to other pages while downloading.

Progress: 0%

- You can then choose to install the Plug-in now or later

Trend Micro Security (for Mac) Download

Trend Micro Security (for Mac) version 1.6.1060 download is complete.

| Install Now | Install Later |

Updating the Plug-in

If an update is available for the plug-in it will now appear where the download button had appeared in the Plug-ins Manager.

Chapter 12 - Security for Mac Plug-in
(As of 1.6.1060)

You will need at least 1.5GB of free disk space. We recommend 2-3GB of free space on the server.

- You will also need the latest Java JRE if you are running on a Windows 2008 server.

Once you have gotten past 40% on the installation, you will know the installation should install correctly and you can go have a cup of coffee. The process will take some time.

You can now click on the **Manage Program** button to enter your activation code. If you do not have an activation code handy, you can click on the evaluation option. This will give you 30 days to try out the program and get a license key.

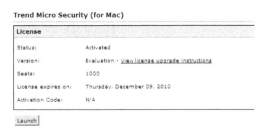

Click the **Launch** button to continue into the program itself. The setup of the Plug-in is much like the setup of WFBS itself. Maybe in the future they will merge into one, but for now we have to open the Plug-in separately and set it up.

Installing Agents

There are a few ways of getting the Agent on the Mac desktop. If you use Apple Remote Desktop, you can quicken the install method. The installation files are re-built every time a configuration change is made to the console. Now, this means a few things:

- Test one or two Agents before going nuts and installing all your Mac systems with WFBS. You cannot make certain changes to the Mac Agents unless you uninstall and re-install the Agent back to the systems. So be careful and test first!
- The installer is downloaded (by the different methods) to the client and it is then installed.
- Changes made after you download will be sent to the Agents when they connect to the Server, but they must connect to the server to get the changes.
- You cannot install a Mac client from the Web Console Login page; this is only for Windows Agents.
- Port 61617 is used by default to communicate to the Agents. Make sure the port is open on your server, both inbound and outbound.
- Configure your server first. Install the clients second; this will make your life much easier.
- The install package is located via the Network:
  https://server-name:4343/SMB/console/html/TMSM_HTML/ActiveUpdate/ClientInstall/tmsminstall.mpkg.zip
- The install package is located via the Server:
  \Program Files\Trend Micro\Security Server\Addon\TMSM\TMSM_HTML\ActiveUpdate\ClientInstall\ tmsminstall.mpkg.zip

So, to install, you need to find a method of getting the install program to the Mac Client. You can use any method you might have of sending/sharing files. Once you get the file to the computers, you can run the file to start the install.

Choose the Drive you want to install the program on.

Depending on your system rights, you will need to use the administrator password to install the program. The install should take about a minute to complete.

Mac Agent

Once it is installed, you will be able to find the Agent in your Applications Finder, or in the *Menu Bar* on the desktop.

Once the Agent communicates to the server, it will allow you access to the program.

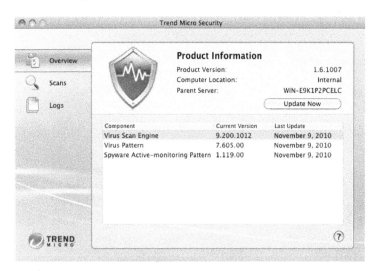

Overview: The Agent shows you which version of the pattern files and engines are installed. You will also be able to *'Update Now'* to the server.

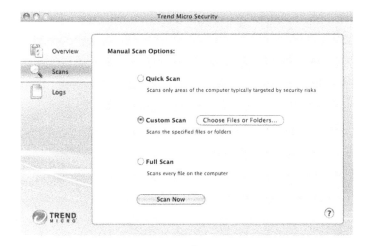

Scans: This allows you to run a scan on your system.

- **Quick Scan**: This looks at the areas that are usually attacked by hackers and the programs they place on your computer. It's a good way of making sure everything is OK.
- **Custom Scan**: Scan a particular part of your computer using the Finder program.

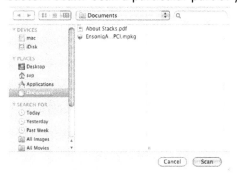

- **Full Scan**: The full scan scans everything on the computer; this scan will take some time.

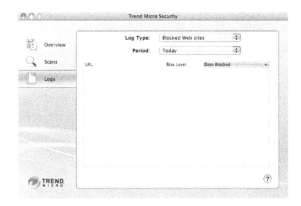

Logs: The log page allows you to see a list of security risks or blocked websites found since the last connection to the server. All log files are uploaded to the server during every connection and deleted from the Agent.

- Quarantined Files: If you choose Security Risks you will also be able to look at any quarantined files that have been found by the Agent. If you select a file you will then be able to delete it or restore it to the computer. If you restore a file, it will be quarantined again during the next scheduled or manual scan of the computer, unless the file is added to the exclusion list on the server.

Uninstalling Clients

At this time, you must uninstall the Mac Client with an uninstall program. You can receive the uninstall program at the same location as in the install file, and it is named *tmsmuninstall.mpkg.zip*.

Summary

Here, you will see a summary of the Mac machines you have installed. Like you could on the WFBS summary screen, you will be able to click on any problems that are shown and figure out what machines the problem is located on.

Client Management

Here, you will be able to see and configure each of our computers and the groups you put them into.

On the right hand side of your screen, you will have listed Default under the Trend Micro Security Server section.

Agents

You can double click on each group to find a list of Agents listed in the group. You will first notice that each Agent is marked as either Online or Offline

Groups

The reason for groups is to divide your agents into configuration groups, or groups of Agents with the same configuration. Examples of good groups are **Laptops, Home Users,** and **Desktops**. Each of these might have different settings. If you have smarter then average users whom you you trust, you may consider a **Nerds** group. As we go through the settings, we will use these groups to explain different reasons for choosing a confguration.

IMPORTANT: In this chapter, when you make configuration changes you will either select a group or an individual Agent. By selecting the *Trend Micro Security Server,* you will select every Mac computer loaded now and that will be installed on the server. When you select a group, the changes we make will go to EVERY machine in that group. By selecting an Individual Agent, you will only be sending the configuration to that one machine. If you make a change to one Agent in the group and then go to the top group and make a change, you will reset that change to all the Agents, including that one you changed individually. The whole group will get the settings, including the individual agent you had already changed. Be careful, and think about how to best use groups.

Add Group

Select Add Group Button to create a new group.

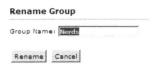

Rename a Group

Click the group you want to rename on the left and select rename group to rename the group. You cannot rename the Default Group (that's useful, isn't it?).

Move a Client

Find and select the Agent(s) you want to move, select Move Client, and select the folder you want to move the Agent to.

- You can choose to either immediately change the Agent's settings to the new group or to wait until the Agent connects to make the changes. No matter what, the Agent will get the settings of the new group.

Removing Group/Client

You can select a group(s) or Agent(s) to remove from the console. Note:

- You cannot remove a group unless all of the Agents are removed from the group first.
- You cannot remove the Default group.
- Removing the Agent will not delete the Agent from the downstream computer. It will simply remove the Agent from the console. If the Agent becomes (or is) active, it will re-appear when the Agent next communicates to the server.
- Agents do NOT automatically remove themselves from the console after being offline for *X* amount of time. You must manage the console by hand to remove Agents you think are no longer running.

Tasks

A Task in the Mac console allows you to either tell the Agent to update or to scan the computer. Do note that the server does not actively run processes on the Agents; it simply sends a message to the Agents asking them to run a process. The Agents will receive that message if they are online on the network, or the next time they connect to the server.

- Update: Tell the Agents there is an update on the server, come and get it.
- Scan Now: Tell the Agents to run a manual scan on the computer (full scan) using the settings you have set under Manual Scan in the console.

Settings

By selecting the top *Trend Micro Security Group*, a group, or an individual Agent, you can set the scanning and Web Reputation settings for those machines.

- If you choose the top *Trend Micro Security Group* you will be asked when you save to the settings to:
    - Apply to All Clients: All the current and future Agents; or
    - Apply to Future Groups Only: The settings will not affect any groups currently listed, but if you make a new group or groups, the settings will be applied to that group(s) by default.

    - We don't make this stuff up, we only explain it.....

Manual Scan Settings:

How are manual scans controlled when run either from the Agent itself or requested by the console?

- **Scan compressed files**: Do you want to scan any compressed files already sitting on the computers? The consideration here is that it takes time to decompress and scan the files inside of a compressed file. If the file is already on the computer, in theory it has already been scanned by the Agent and should be safe. But odds are, if you are doing a manual scan, you are worried about something being wrong on the computers you are scanning. For this reason, we recommend selecting this option on all your agents.

- **CPU Usage**: How much computer time do you want to take up during a scan? This question really has to do with why you are scanning the computes in the first place. If you are scanning because you are in an emergency, then use High Utilization. If you are scanning just for fun, then take Low Utilization.

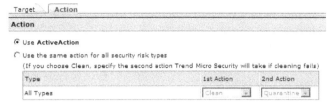

- **ActiveAction:** In the Actions tab, you will tell WFBS what to do when it encounters a problem. The default setting (letting WFBS decide) is ActiveAction. In the last ten years, viruses have become un-cleanable. Back in the 1990's, viruses would try to infect a single file. Those files were sometimes cleanable, and you could actually use the file after cleaning the virus out of it. As virus writers have progressed, they no longer look into infecting single files, but have progressed into infecting your process DLLs and EXEs. So Trend Micro has developed a system that determines by each infection type how to deal with the files infected. Some clients have found these settings to not correctly find and delete new infections and use the manual configuration noted below to setup their Agents. We recommend using Active Action if you're not sure about what options to choose and want to take the safe and simple option.
- **Choose your actions:** Here, you can decide what you are going to do with all the problems WFBS finds. There is a first action and a second action. The first action should always be clean, and we would say the second option should always be delete. But if you want to quarantine as a second choice, feel free.

Real-time Scan Settings

Real-time scanning is what WFBS does, on the fly to find problems. Here, you have a choice of how to look at files and notifcations of information to the user.

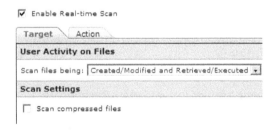

- When should you scan? You have to decide when you want to scan files going through the computer. We recommend by default choosing Created/Modified as it will do the best job at checking data, but only when the data is touched.
    - **Creating a file**: Any process can create a file on your computer. You don't see all the processes running on your computer unless you look. Check them out yourself if you like: *Ctrl-Alt-Delete ->Task Manager -> Processes*. There is a list of every process your

machine is running. Each of these has the right to make a file. How do you know if a hacker breaks into a program, and tells the program to start writing files (with a virus) to your computer? You don't. So check every file created on your computer.

- o **Modify a file**: Almost the same as creating a file, any process on your computer can open, modify and save a file. Many spyware programs are known to take good current files and turn them into virus seeds.   This should also be checked all the time.
- o **Retrieving/Executing a file**: OK, so you have the files on your computer taken care of, but what happens if you get a file from a server, or your email, or the Internet?   These files must be scanned while you retrieve them before we put them on our computer.

- **Scan compressed files**: Do you want to scan any compressed files already sitting on the computers? The consideration here is that it takes time to decompress and scan the files inside of a compressed file. If the file is already on the computer, in theory it has already been scanned by the Agent and should be safe. But odds are, if you are doing a manual scan , you are worried about something being wrong on the computers you are scanning. For this reason, we recommend selecting this option on all your agents.

- **ActiveAction:** In the Actions tab we will tell WFBS what to do when we encounter a problem. The default setting (Letting WFBS decide) is ActiveAction.   In the last ten years, viruses have become un-cleanable. Back in the 1990's viruses would try to infect a single file. Those files were sometimes cleanable, and you could actually use the file after cleaning the virus out of it. As virus writers have progressed, they no longer look into infecting single files, but have progressed into infecting your process DLLs and EXEs. So Trend Micro has developed a system that determines by each infection type how to deal with the files infected.   Some clients have found these settings to not correctly find and delete new infections and use the manual configuration noted below to setup their Agents. We recommend using Active Action if you're not sure about what options to choose and want to take the safe and simple option.
- **Choose your actions:** Here, you can decide what you are going to do with all the problems the system finds.   You can select a first action and a second action. The first action should always be clean, and we would say the second option should always be delete. But if you want to quarantine as a second choice, feel free.
- **Display a message on the Desktop:** Do you want the user to know if a problem was found on their computer or not? This really depends on your users and how they react to problems. We have some customers who have different groups for people who can handle the notification and a group for people they know would handle the information the wrong way.

Scheduled Scan

- **Schedule**: You are only allowed to create one scheduled scan for each group. You can choose how often and at what time to start a scheduled scan. If your users leave their machines on overnight you should probably do your scan at night. If they turn them off at night, consider scanning at lunch time.

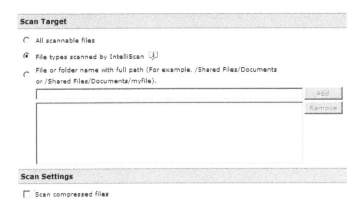

- **All Scannable Files.** Simply put, if it can be scanned (it's not encrypted in some way) we will scan it, every time it moves, is opened, is saved. Everything all the time.

- **IntelliScan.** Instead of looking at the file extensions (.bat, .exe, .doc....)while scanning, we will look inside the file header to figure out what it the file really is. This is set as the Default setting and unless you have a reason should remain so.

> *Inside IntelliScan*
>
> *Not every file is as it seems. Every file has an extension. This enables Windows to determine what program should run the program. .doc files are for a word processor. .exe files are executables. But anyone can change these extensions and therefore break how Windows starts a program. How/Why? Maybe you have worked for a company that didn't let you email pictures. To get around it you could simply rename the file from .jpg to .abc. The email system is only looking for picture file extension .jpg; since .abc isn't blocked it lets the file go. In the email you tell the person on the other end to change the extension back to .jpg to use it. IntelliScan looks inside of every file it scans for the header, the header which tells the WFBS more about the file then just what an extension is. In the header you will see stuff like what kind of file it is, when it was created, how big it should be.... IntelliScan allows you to stop your users from breaking the system by changing extensions, and more importantly, stops hackers from hiding bad programs behind the mask of a simple and boring file extension.*

- **File or Folder**: If you have a distinct file or folder you would like to scan regularly, you can select a group of them here. The only problem with this option is that you cannot create a scheduled scan for the whole drive AND one for specific files or folders. You have to select one or the other (or create special groups for them).

- **Scan compressed files**: Do you want to scan any compressed files already sitting on the computers? The consideration here is that it takes time to decompress and scan the files inside of a compressed file. If the file is already on the computer, in theory it has already been scanned by the Agent and should be safe. But odds are, if you are doing a manual scan, you are worried about something being wrong on the computers you are scanning. For this reason, we recommend selecting this option on all your agents.

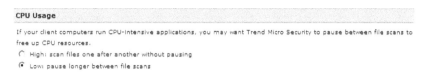

- **CPU Usage**: All scheduled scans should always be run at low CPU Usage.

- **ActiveAction:** In the Actions tab, you will tell WFBS what to do when it encounters a problem. The default setting (Letting WFBS decide) is ActiveAction. In the last ten years, viruses have become un-cleanable. Back in the 1990's viruses would try to infect a single file. Those files were sometimes cleanable, and you could actually use the file after cleaning the virus out of it. As Virus writers have progressed, they no longer look into infecting single files, but have progressed into infecting your process DLLs and EXEs. So Trend Micro has developed a system that determines by each infection type how to deal with the files infected. Some clients have found these settings to not correctly find and delete new infections and use the manual configuration noted below to setup their Agents. We recommend using Active Action if you're not sure about what options to choose and want to take the safe and simple option.
- **Choose your actions:** Here, you can decide what you are going to do with all the problems the system finds. You can choose a first action and a second action. The first action should always be clean, and we would say the second option should always be delete. But if you want to quarantine as a second choice, feel free.
- **Postpone or Cancel:** Should you allow your users to postpone or (worse) cancel scheduled scans? We would only recommend this for your very smartest users. Postponing or canceling a scheduled scan could quickly turn into a bad situation.

Scan Exclusions

Are there files you want to exclude?

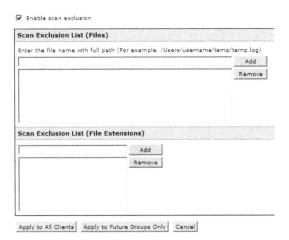

- **File Names:** There are also files you won't want scanned. What you should be interested in here is if WFBS does anything funky with a program you run on some or all of your desktops. The best example I have seen over the years is either your human resource or your accounting programs. These programs are notorious for doing funky things with databases and how they run on your computer. If you have these problems determined by yourself or with Trend Micro's help, you can put them in here.
- **File Extensions:** Excluding file extensions is a bit more dangerous. Here, you would be overwriting the IntelliScan option you set above by saying "never scan any file with the following extension, even if it is another program hiding as this extension." Again, if you find a program or file type that is being a problem, put it in here, but don't do that unless you are sure that it is the problem.

Dale Johnson

Web Reputation

Like you could in the firewall settings, you can set up Web Reputation separately for in the office and out of the office. Web Reputation allows you to stop your users from going to known bad websites. These websites can have viruses, security risks, and/or Trojans. You can turn on Web Reputation for internal (desktops that can see the server) and/or external (desktops that cannot see the server and must be out of the office) machines. We recommend always turning on Web Reputation both in and out of the office; you never know where your users are going online or how that will affect your computer when it's back in the office.

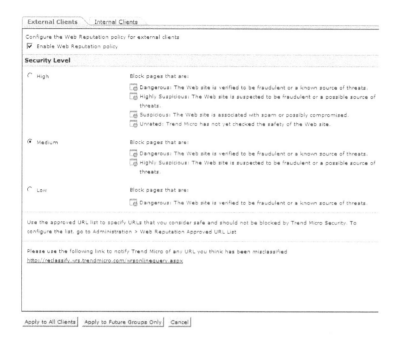

Trend Micro maintains a database of websites that it considers to have reputations (bad ones for this purpose). They have divided those sites up for WFBS in the following categories:

- **Verified fraud pages or threat sources:** These are known web sites and pages that have a virus, spyware, or such attached to them. If you go there, you will have a problem.
- **Suspected fraud pages or threat sources:** These sites have been found to have problems but have a lower rating as either the problems with the site aren't full time or some people consider the threat OK (like a screensaver program). It is probably best to try this setting and see if your users complain about not going to these sites.
- **Associated with spam or possibly compromised:** These sites are from known spammers or maybe have been compromised due to the web system they are running. Certain types of websites are less secure then others; these sites are in the very unsecure zone and either can be or have been compromised. Choosing this option will block some sites your users might actually use. Sadly lots of websites are ignored by their webmasters. They have been left alone or the webmasters don't care to secure them.
- **Unrated pages:** This mostly consists of new pages that simply haven't been rated. A webpage needs to be searched or used by Trend Micro's clients and its internal servers before it gets a

rating. You should probably not use this option for your users; the web grows by so many pages a day that your users will come across new pages often enough to make this a bit annoying.

Can you see the pages listed in these groups? No. Trend Micro keeps the database secure so that the hackers that make these sites won't know that they have been found. You can search individual web sites using their reclassification tool at http://reclassify.wrs.trendmicro.com/ if you wish. You can also tell Trend Micro about websites you either want to add to the database or sites you want them to take off the database. This webpage can only be used by administrators and will make you enter your license key to ensure that only Trend Micro clients are doing updates.

Log Files

You can search the uploaded Agent log files to see what has happened over a set amount of time. There are no reports in the Mac Security Plug-in at the time, so this is the only way of getting log information from the Agents. The setup for both Security Risks and Web Reputation log searches are the same.

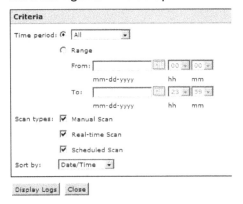

- Time Period: Select when you want to do your search. The speed of the search is directly related to how much time you select to cover in your search. Also, you are limited in the search by how long you keep log files. By default, you keep 30 days of log files.
- Scan Type: Do you want information about Manual, Real-time, or Scheduled Scans?
- Sort: How do you want the output sorted? Options include:
  o Date/Time
  o Computer
  o Security Risk
  o Source
  o Scan Type
  o Result
  o Platform

Server Updates

Manual Updates

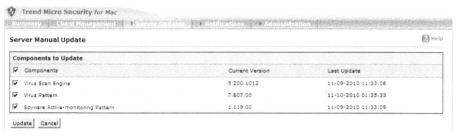

Select which items you would like to update and click the *Update* button.

Scheduled Update

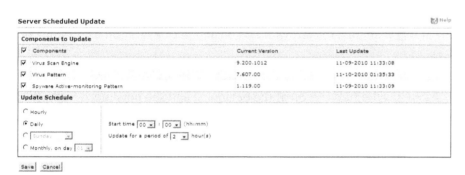

Along with selecting which items you would like to regularly schedule, you can also choose how often you would like them updated. We recommend selecting hourly.

Update Source

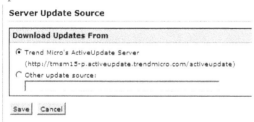

If you have more than one WFBS server, you can choose to have one update and have the rest of the servers update from that one server. This is very useful if you have many offices, but only one with an Internet connection. You can type in a FTP or Share location to find the updated Scan Engines and Pattern Files.

Notifications

The question you will ask yourself in this section is: how much do you want to hear about from the WFBS server about Mac problems? Most people will select the most critical notifications, ignoring the day-to-day notifications, which would be background noise after a few days. Do note that these notifications are just for the Mac installed agents and do not combine with the Windows side of WFBS (sadly).

Standard Notifications

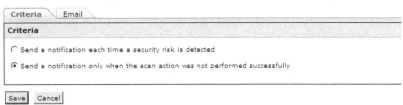

- **Send notification each time**: Do you want a notification every time an event happens, or every time any virus is found? It might be best to start with this on and decide later on if you want all the traffic it creates.
- **Send notification on bad scan action**: Do you want a notification every time a virus is not cleaned successfully? Again, maybe turn this on at the beginning and see how much traffic it produces.

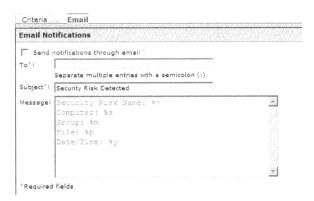

- The only option is to send the notification though email, so here, you can choose the person or group to send it to, along with creating your own message and subject line. Clicking *Select notification though email is* the way of turning these alerts on and off.

Dale Johnson

Outbreak Notifications

Configure Trend Micro Security to send notifications to administrator when an outbreak occurs.

Criteria | Email

Criteria

☐ Unique sources:

Detections: 100

Time period: 24 hour(s)

Save Cancel

A much better way of getting notifications is using Outbreak Analysis, which you can configure if notifications occur when multiple events happen. You will be combining these options in an AND Boolean statement. So we are looking for events happening on a certain amount of Agents AND a certain amount of events AND during a certain time period.

- Unique Sources: If events happens on *X* amount of machines during the period.
- Detections: How many total events, including actually finding a virus, happen during the period?
- What period of time should you consider the event duration.

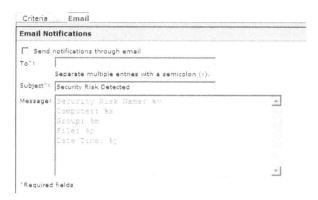

Criteria | Email

Email Notifications

☐ Send notifications through email

To*:

Separate multiple entries with a semicolon (;).

Subject*: Security Risk Detected

Message: Security Risk Name: %v
Computer: %s
Group: %m
File: %p
Date/Time: %y

*Required fields

- The only option is to send the notification though email, so here, you can choose the person or group to send it to, along with creating your own message and subject line. Clicking *Select notification though email is* the way of turning these alerts on and off.

General Settings

Email Notifications

SMTP server:

Port Number: 25

From:

* Specify an email address in the format someone@example.com.

Save Cancel

Place your Mail server information, along with an email address to use as a return address (it does not have to be a real account; think about something like *wfbs-mac alerts@...*)

Administration

Client Setup Files

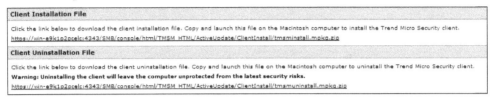

Client Installation File

Click the link below to download the client installation file. Copy and launch this file on the Macintosh computer to install the Trend Micro Security client.

https://win-e9k1p2pcelc:4343/SMB/console/html/TMSM_HTML/ActiveUpdate/ClientInstall/tmsminstall.mpkg.zip

Client Uninstallation File

Click the link below to download the client uninstallation file. Copy and launch this file on the Macintosh computer to uninstall the Trend Micro Security client.

Warning: Uninstalling the client will leave the computer unprotected from the latest security risks.

https://win-e9k1p2pcelc:4343/SMB/console/html/TMSM_HTML/ActiveUpdate/ClientInstall/tmsmuninstall.mpkg.zip

This gives you a link and more information about how to find the Client Install and Uninstall files. As mentioned before, the Install file is updated EVERY TIME you make a change in the Mac Security Console.

Client-Server Communication

If you need to configure the server name/IP address, listening port, and proxy server settings, conf
clients and then change any of these settings, clients will lose connection with the server and the or

Server Name and Listening Port

Server name (or IP address): [   ] [Add]

Server Names/IP Addresses	
192.168.159.128	🗑

Port number*: [61617]

*Changes to the port number will apply to all server names/IP addresses.

When you installed the Plug-in, the install program took data from the server to determine how to communicate with the server. It used the first IP address as the default IP address along with the default port (61617) in the setup. For most people, this would not be a problem, but you may want to use either a DNS entry or another IP address on the server instead of the default settings.

BIG GOTCHA: If you make a change to the server IP address and/or port and you have installed Agents, those Agents WILL NOT be able to connect again to the server and there is (at this point) no way of changing the Mac Agent to fix the problem. You will have to uninstall and reinstall (with the new installer program) the Mac Agents in order to get them to work.

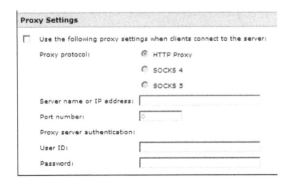

Proxy Settings

☐ Use the following proxy settings when clients connect to the server:

Proxy protocol: ◉ HTTP Proxy
                 ○ SOCKS 4
                 ○ SOCKS 5

Server name or IP address: [   ]

Port number: [0]

Proxy server authentication:

User ID: [   ]

Password: [   ]

If you use a proxy server between the Server and the Clients, you can setup the proxy information here.

External Proxy Settings

Proxy Settings

☐ Use the following proxy settings when clients connect to the server:

Proxy protocol:
- ⦿ HTTP Proxy
- ○ SOCKS 4
- ○ SOCKS 5

Server name or IP address: [_____]

Port number: [0]

Proxy server authentication:

User ID: [_____]

Password: [_____]

If you have a proxy between the WFBS server and the Internet, you can input that data here.

Web Reputation Approved URL List

Approved URL List

Enter approved URL:

http:// [_____] [Add >>]

* Wildcard character is supported

Approved URL	
http://c.microsoft.com/*	🗑
http://download.microsoft.com/*	🗑
http://download.windowsupdate.com/*	🗑
http://housecall.antivirus.com/*	🗑
http://kb.trendmicro.com/*	🗑

If you have websites you would like to not block users from surfing on the Internet, you can add them into this section. Do note that if you approve a website all webpages and sub-sites will also be accessible (in other words if you add *www.jconsult.com* you will also be allowing *www.jconsult/inside-wfbs*). You can also delete currently listed websites by clicking on the little trash can next to the listed site.

Log Maintenance

☑ Enable scheduled deletion of logs

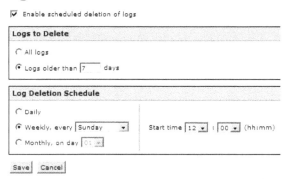

Logs to Delete

○ All logs
⦿ Logs older than [7] days

Log Deletion Schedule

○ Daily
⦿ Weekly, every [Sunday ▾]   Start time [12 ▾] : [00 ▾] (hh:mm)
○ Monthly, on day [01 ▾]

[Save] [Cancel]

Here, you will automatically delete the Mac Security log files from the WFBS server. By default, the system is set to delete any log file older than 7 days old every Sunday night at midnight. We recommend (if you have the disk space) going to 30 days on the log files. If you are having problems with disk space, you may want to change the deletion time to daily instead of weekly.

Product License

Here, you can look at the current license you have installed

- **Update Information**: You can check the Internet if you want to update the expiration date after renewing the license.
- **New Activation Code**: You can put in a new activation key if you are upgrading from an evaluation or if you get a new activation key from Trend Micro.
- **View detailed license online**: This will bring you to the Trend Micro Online Registration web page (olr.trendmicro.com) to log into your Registration account in order to look at your license detail.

Troubleshooting

Here we will discuss answers and fixes to the most asked questions we have seen in WFBS.

Hints and Tricks

What does Behavior Monitoring Monitor?

Duplicated System File: System files (mostly contained in the Windows/System32 directory) are supposed to be limited to the processes that use them. Hackers love to take these files and replace them with their own files, so that when they are called by the process they will go and do something bad. This setting will monitor your system files, watching for the wrong programs attempting to write, replace, or appending your good files. Trend Micro maintains a database of files and which programs should be working with them. The only negative might be if you have a strange office program (that Trend Micro doesn't have in its database) that might go and play with these files while it runs. We have the ability later on in this section to exclude files we know might be a problem. We recommend that you use this option (ask first, then when you feel good going to always block) and if you find problems, exclude the problem files

Host Files Modification: Each Windows machine has a *Hosts*. (no extension located in the windows\system32\drivers\etc directory) file. This file allows you to hard code a DNS name as an IP address.

- An internal example is to hard coded your WFBS Host name as the IP address like :
  - 192.168.93.1   dale-f00d7db216.jcvmware.local
- We can also use the Hosts. files for browsing the Internet. An example is to have a two company websites, one for your internal users and one for the rest of the world. Using the Hosts. You can point your internal users to the internal website every time they trying going to your website. Like:
  - 68.164.219.157   www.jconsult.com

So, you can see that a hacker can do a lot of things if he gets to the Hosts. file. We highly recommend using this option in always block mode to stop access to this file.

Suspicious Behavior: Hackers tend to do things that the average user doesn't normally do on their machine. An Example: Your users rarely write to the registry followed by editing a file in the windows directory. In fact, I hope they never do that. Trend Micro has created a set of commands and actions, that when combined with other commands and actions, trigger an alert that something strange is going on. We recommend turning this option on, using always block if your users have average user intelligence and ask if you have a nerdier group than normal.

New Internet Explorer Plugin: Ah, Internet Explorer, the hacker's dream. It is so easy to place plugins into IE that it's plain scary. A plugin can do lots of things. They can watch where you go, read data typed in, send you to bad websites, or simply blurt out advertisements every few seconds. It's so easy to get it done, that Trend Micro now monitors the registry for changes being added to IE. You should either place this on ask (if you don't mind your users adding endless toolbars and plugins) or block all the time (to stop such annoyances from going on your machines completely).

Internet Explorer Setting Modifications: Like the Hosts. file, there are other ways to change your internet settings. Most of this is done with the registry, so Trend Micro watches for additions to the registry and a few configuration files to make sure things don't get added without you knowing. We recommend this is turned on to always block.

Security Policy Modification: Windows maintains its own security policies that stop a user from doing certain things or sharing certain folders or files. Trend Micro will monitor the policy set to make sure it is not changed. We highly recommend this to be turned on with always block as the only option.

Program Library Injection: When a Windows program needs to call a smaller program, it runs a DLL (Dynamic Link Library) file. Hackers like to either change the DLLs so that when they are called they do something bad, or change the programs so that they call the wrong or extra DLLs. WFBS checks writing to DLLs and EXEs to make sure they aren't compromised. We highly recommend this be set to always block.

Shell Modification: Windows shell is the graphical interface of a computer. It calls programs when something needs to be run on the monitor. These calls can be hacked to run extra programs (that the hacker places on your computer) without you ever noticing. WFBS checks the shell settings to make sure that nothing is changed. We recommend setting this to always block.

New Service: When a program runs in the background (all the time) on a computer, it is considered a service. You can see a list of services by running typing *services.msc* in *Start -> Run*. There is nothing stopping anyone from creating their own service and having it run their program all the time on your computer. It can be done with a few simple registry settings. WFBS will watch the services section of the registry and make sure nothing is written to it. Because users (and you) do install programs that create services, we recommend setting this to ask.

System File Modification: WFBS is here watching your basic windows settings: screensavers, background pictures, startup programs and the like. It will make sure they are only changed by the user, in the correct locations. We recommend keeping this on always block.

Firewall Policy Modification: WFBS monitors the Windows firewall and its network settings to make sure they are not changed by a hacker's program. Since there are programs (The WFBS Agent is one of them) that will need to edit the Windows firewall, we should set this to ask.

System Process Modification: Each program currently running on your computer runs a process. You can see the processes by running *taskmgr.exe* in *Start -> Run*. WFBS will check running processes and make sure they are not stopped or modified (restarted as a different process). A good example of this happening is when a hacker drops a fake antivirus program onto your computer. The first thing it attempts to do is stop your current antivirus process. Once it has stopped it, it can then do anything on your computer (and does). Since processes start and stop routinely on your computer, we recommend keeping turned onto always allow. Use it when you know you have a problem, turn it to ask then you will see what's happening on an infected computer.

New Startup Programs: A program can be either put in the startup folder of your start -> programs or it can be written into the auto start section of your registry. This will watch the registry for additions to auto starts. We recommend keeping this on ask, since new programs will ask to be added to this area.

Trouble Downloading Pattern Files onto server:

If you have problems downloading pattern files onto the server from Trend Micro, you can get a little more information on what is wrong from the TMUDUMP.TXT log file. The file is located in:

C:\Program Files\Trend Micro\Security Server\PCCSRV\Web\Service\AU_Data\AU_Log

Corrupted Pattern Files on server:

- First, rollback your pattern files one version; see chapter 6.
- Then, delete the current pattern file in either of these directories (depending on which file is corrupted).

C:\Program Files\Trend Micro\Security Server\PCCSRV
C:\Program Files\Trend Micro\Security Server\PCCSRV\download

Corrupted SmartScan pattern files on server:

Since these files are special, it is easiest to search for the solution in the Trend Micro knowledge base with the word "TBLPtnImportTool".

Pattern Files taking up too much space on Agents:

If your pattern files are taking too much space on your workstations you should consider using Smart Scanning. See Chapter 7.

I'm running out of disk space on my server:

Use the Disk Cleaner to clean up old data either manually or automated. See chapter 6.

How can I keep fewer pattern files on my server and use less disk space?

Too many patterns file are filling my hard drive!   We usually keep old pattern files in case we need to roll back from a new one, but we really don't need too many of them.

To make the change:

In explorer go to the folder
C:\Program Files\Trend Micro\Security Server\PCCSRV\wss

- Edit *UpdatePattern.ini*
- Find the section named *[GenBFDiff]*
- The default setting is: *MaxDiff=24, KeepPtn=7*
- You can set both of these lower. Trend Micro recommends *MaxDiff=12, KeepPtn=4*
- Save and close the file.
- The next time a pattern update happens; the process will check to the file and clean up as directed.

Some or all of my Agents have disappeared from my server:

Have all or some of your agents disappeared from your server?   It could be a corrupted database.   Here is the fix.

- Stop the **Trend Micro Security Server Master Service**

  Trend Micro Messaging Security Agent Master Service   Messaging ...   Started   Automatic
- Rename the following directory:
  C:\Program Files\Trend Micro\Security Server\PCCSRV\HTTPDB
  to
  C:\Program Files\Trend Micro\Security Server\PCCSRV\HTTPDB-old
- Create A new folder called
  C:\Program Files\Trend Micro\Security Server\PCCSRV\HTTPDB
- Start the **Trend Micro Security Server Master Service**

  Trend Micro Messaging Security Agent Master Service   Messaging ...   Started   Automatic
- Now you can either wait for the Agents to contact the server (this should be within three hours or less), or you can go to each machine and restart the Trend Micro Client/Server Security Agent Listener service on each machine.

  Trend Micro Client/Server Security Agent Listener   Receives c...   Started   Automatic

If none of this works, try to use the Regenerate an Agent GUID tool in the Tools Chapter.

I need to move the server to another drive on the server:

To move the server to another drive we will have to reinstall it using the backed-up data. This is no easy task, so make sure you have enough disk space to begin with.

The steps are:

- Stop the **Trend Micro Security Server Master Service**

  Trend Micro Messaging Security Agent Master Service   Messaging ...   Started   Automatic

- You can get these your port numbers by searching your ofcscan.ini file from

  C:\Program Files\Trend Micro\Security Server\PCCSRV

  - Master_DomainName=
  - Master_DomainPort=
  - Client_LocalServer_Port=

- Backup the following directory:

  C:\Program Files\Trend Micro\Security Server\PCCSRV\HTTPDB

- If you are using the MSA, you will need to uninstall it via the Security Settings section.

- Uninstall the WFBS Agent from the server via **Add/Remove Programs**

- Uninstall WFBS from the server via **Add/Remove Programs**

- Reinstall WFBS

- Stop the **Trend Micro Security Server Master Service**

  Trend Micro Messaging Security Agent Master Service   Messaging ...   Started   Automatic

- Replace this current folder with the one you backed-up

  C:\Program Files\Trend Micro\Security Server\PCCSRV\HTTPDB

- Start the **Trend Micro Security Server Master Service**

  Trend Micro Messaging Security Agent Master Service   Messaging ...   Started   Automatic

- Reinstall the MSA

- Take a long vacation

I can't get in my web console, or when I do it looks all messed up:

If, when using IIS 6.0, you can't get into your web console at all (even after following our installation page); or when you do, you do not see the pages correctly, you might possibly need to rebuild your WFBS website. You can do this by following these steps:

- Open your IIS manager: Start -> Program Files -> Administrative Tools -> Internet Information Services (IIS) Manager

- Find the OfficeScan virtual site INSIDE of the OfficeScan website and right-click, then select Properties and Delete. DO NOT DELETE THE WHOLE OfficeScan WEB SITE ITSELF!!!!!   We are looking for OfficeScan Virtual Site inside the OfficeScan website. Your OfficeScan website should now look like:

- Exit out of IIS Manager for now
- Go to a command prompt (Start -> Run -> CMD) , and change directory (CD) to \Program Files\Trend Micro\Security Server\PCCSRV

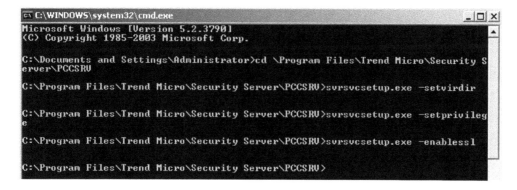

- Run the following commands, in order, depending on if you're running 32bit or 64 bit
  - svrsvcsetup.eXE –uninstall   or   svrsvcsetup_64x.eXE – uninstall
  - svrsvcsetup.eXE –install   or   svrsvcsetup_64x.eXE –install
  - svrsvcsetup.eXE –setvirdir   or   svrsvcsetup_64x.eXE –setvirdir
  - svrsvcsetup.eXE –setprivilege   or   svrsvcsetup_64x.eXE –setprivilege
  - svrsvcsetup.eXE –enablessl   or   svrsvcsetup_64x.eXE –enablessl
- Now go back into IIS Manager and find the OfficeScan website -> right click -> Properties .

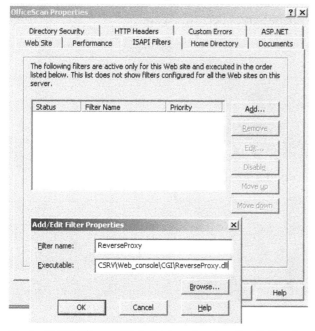

- Go to ISAPI Filters, Click Add and enter the following information:
  - ReverseProxy
  - C:\Program Files\Trend Micro\Security Server\PCCSRV\Web_console\CGI\ReverseProxy.dll
- Get out of IIS, and now you should be able to use your console. Rarely, you might have to reboot to get it all to work. If you can't, then something else is wrong and it's time to contact Trend Micro Support.

How do I find my version numbers?

On the Console

- Log into the console
- Go to Help, About from the top tabs

- The screen will now tell you what SP level and what build number you are at on the Server

On the Agent

- Right click on the Agent icon at the bottom of the screen or go to Start -> Programs -> Trend Micro Client-Server Security Agent -> Client-Server Security Agent

- Select the *Help* Tab and click on the link under *About* called *more info*

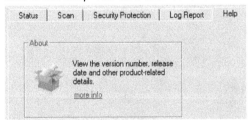

- Your product version will appear on the screen

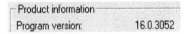

Dale Johnson

What Ports do I have to drill into my firewall?

Between WFBS and Trend Micro (the internet):

- Port 25 if you are connecting to an outside mail server.
- Port 80 to get pattern file updates.

Between your Agents and WFBS, find the port values inside your
C:\Program Files\Trend Micro\Security Server\PCCSR\OfcScan.ini

- Master_DomainPort=
- Client_LocalServer_Port=

Between your Exchange Server and WFBS:

- Port 16732

Between your administrator (You) and your WFBS:

- Port 4343

Index

Johnson Consulting, Inc.

www.jconsult.com/inside

21 Parliament Lane
Woburn MA 01801

877-228-8595
info@jconsult.com

www.ingramcontent.com/pod-product-compliance
Lightning Source LLC
Chambersburg PA
CBHW080359060326
40689CB00019B/4074